First Nations 101

Lynda Gray

Adaawx Publishing

3rd Printing, 2013

Adaawx Publishing
P.O. Box 44502
Vancouver, British Columbia
Canada V5L 4R8

'Adaawx' is a Sm'algyax (language of the Tsimshian) word that when translated as closely as possible to English means 'oral history' or 'truth telling'

ISBN 978-0-9869640-0-8

Written and published within the traditional, unceded territories of the Musqueam, Squamish, and Tsleil-Waututh Nations

Printed and bound in Canada by Friesens

$1.00 from the sale of every First Nations 101 book will be donated to the Urban Native Youth Association's capital campaign to build a Native Youth Centre in Vancouver, B.C.

www.firstnations101.com

Visit www.firstnations101.com to find out more about the author, tour dates, how to book a workshop or presentation, or to order *First Nations 101* directly from the publisher.

Contents

Chapter 3 – Community Issues

Chapter 4 – Fairness & Justice

Chapter 5 – Health & Wellness

Chapter 6 – Arts

Chapter 7 – The Road Forward: Forging A New Path

For Robin and Phil

You inspire me and give me great hope
for our future generations

Introduction

First Nations 101 is my contribution in helping to restore First Nations communities to our former healthy, independent, and proud selves and to move towards reconciliation between First Nations and non-First Nations people. While our struggle to overcome the many social issues we face due to assimilation policies seems overwhelming, and reconciliation with non-First Nations people sometimes seems improbable, I am not willing to just stand by and wait for things to change. Just as the hummingbird would not abandon the burning forest in Michael Nicoll Yahgulanaas' *Flight of the Humming Bird*, I will do what I can regardless of what others are willing to do in the face of such daunting tasks. In our struggle to reclaim the beliefs and traditions of our ancestors, our Elders remind us that we are responsible to the next seven generations, so we must make decisions and act with their best interest in mind.

There have been a few significant conversations that have led to the writing of this book. About 10 years ago, a relative and I who were both in university at the time, talked about how aggravating it was to constantly have to educate or re-educate people about First Nations issues. This is especially annoying within a classroom setting where one would assume that the professors have up-to-date and accurate information to share with their students. This was often not the case. I believe that if an educator is going to raise a particular subject in their classroom they have a responsibility to provide accurate and unbiased information, to positively address any comments or questions that are raised by students, and to not allow racist, derogatory, or other negative remarks to go unchallenged in front of the rest of the class. My relative and I both agreed that, although we were there to be 'educated' and did not like to have to spend lots of time constantly (re)educating people about First Nations issues, as First Nations people we have a responsibility to work towards positive changes for our community. Surely it is not fair that educating the public about First Nations history, people, and concerns is left for First Nations people to do, but it is a burden that we are willing to help carry. We both believe that educating people is one of the best ways to foster widespread and long-lasting positive change, especially since many First Nations issues have been caused by and/or perpetuated by external forces. My comment to my relative was that I felt like I was an ambassador for our people, as I was always trying to change the misguided perception of our community in the eyes of non-First Nations people. As an ambassador, I will not holler at a bigot; rather, I will talk to them or others who are willing to listen and spread the truth like seeds in a field that will take strong root.

The writing of *First Nations 101* happened to coincide with recent significant events, including the 2008 Government of Canada apology to the survivors of Indian residential schools, a few provinces talking about reconciliation, the formation of the Truth and Reconciliation Commission of Canada, and U.S. President Barack Obama's promise of a new relationship with Native Americans. These four things have piqued the interest of many North Americans. The land title question, large urban migration of First Nations people, and the current economic crisis force the average person to confront issues that they might otherwise ignore, including competition for resources with First Nations people. This confluence of events provides a unique opportunity to inform people about First Nations issues and concerns. I believe that if we do not agree with much of the information that is out in the world about First Nations people, then we need to be willing to do something about it. Rather than complaining that people are ignorant about First Nations people, I am choosing to do something to counteract it. Ignorance is not the same as being brainless or unintelligent; rather, to be ignorant is to have a lack of knowledge about something. To counteract ignorance, we must educate.

First Nations 101 is a primer or introductory course about First Nations issues. It is not meant to be a research paper, all inclusive, or an essay. It is meant to highlight the many diverse subjects that affect our lives on a daily basis. I have strove to not only offer my personal opinion, but I have also included statistics and examples so you can form your own opinion. I do not profess to know all the answers, to speak for the diverse range of First Nations people, or to be an authority on any of these issues. Rather, I simply wish to share the little that I know to help inform others so that they can do further research on their own, and therefore make life easier for First Nations people now and in the future. Although as a First Nations woman I seemingly live my life in the margins of a Euro-centric world, like bell hooks I choose to claim that space as "a site of resistance – as [a] location of radical openness and possibility."

I know that *First Nations 101* is not the be all and end all of changing people's views on First Nations people, and many people will not read it, but it is a place to start. It has taken me decades to learn what I know about our history, challenges, and strengths. Hopefully *First Nations 101* will make it easier for others to learn also. Some might assume that First Nations people do not need to read this book as we are already aware of these issues. However, being immersed in the issues and knowing about them and what causes them are two very different things. Most First Nations people do not know much of this information as we have been forcibly separated from our history, traditions, teachings, families, and independence — and many of these truths are not shared in the mainstream school system. This has left many of us struggling just to survive, not being able to thrive as our ancestors did. This reality inhibits us from learning about all of the issues that affect our lives. So I believe that First Nations people can greatly benefit from learning new things about our own history and community. The more I learn, the more empowered I feel to fight against injustice and for our rights as Indigenous people, and to restore our communities to our former healthy, independent, and proud selves.

Several semi-surprising things occurred during the writing of this book. First, every time I told a First Nations person that I was writing this book and what it was about, they were very excited as they immediately recognized the far-reaching benefits of having so much information in one place for people to learn more about our issues and concerns. While *First Nations 101* is meant for the general public, the comments I have received thus far indicate that it would also be useful for secondary and post-secondary schools, government employees, and those participating in training or workshops related to First Nations issues, racism, or cross-cultural understanding.

Second, almost every First Nations person immediately said, "you're going to talk about this subject right?" It wasn't really a suggestion, but more of an affirmation that as a First Nations person I would most certainly have thought about the subject they mentioned. But they had to check it out, just in case. Just like I would have. Most people immediately suggested at least two of the following four issues: 1) Not all First Nations are the same, 2) we do pay taxes, 3) what people should refer to First Nations people as, and 4) the land bridge theory is not true. Everyone felt as passionately as I do that these four issues had to be in the book. The overall confirmation that these subjects must be in the book speaks to the impact that they have on many First Nations people. From this recurring theme, one could assume that most First Nations people come up against questions or comments about these four subjects from non-First Nations people on a regular-enough basis to make it stand out for each of us.

And finally, writing this book has been very cathartic for me. With some subjects I would begin to get angry as I wrote because I knew how wrong people's actions and perceptions about us were, but then I would start to feel good as I knew I was doing something positive about it that could make people think again about what they believe, do, or say in relation to First Nations people. When talking with people over the years and answering their questions about First Nations people, I have received consistent feedback that the information I shared was new to them and that they wished there was a way to learn more and/or to educate someone close to them as most of the books available were not what they were looking for. Since people often believe what their family and friends tell them, I encourage you to share what you learn about First Nations people with others so that they can speak from a place of knowing, not just opinion, hearsay, or speculation.

For the purposes of this book, I will only use the term First Nations which includes all First Nations, Aboriginal, Native, Status, Non-Status, Inuit, and Métis people. Each chapter will focus on a particular theme with several subject entries which may also include a short list of resources at the end so that you can continue your learning after reading *First Nations 101.* Thank you for picking up this book.

Class Syllabus

In order to fully understand First Nations people's current reality, we need to understand the history of what has happened since non-First Nations people first came to our shores. Once you know this information, you will better understand how First Nations people have come to face many social issues today. You will also have a greater appreciation for the great strength that it took for our ancestors to survive the constant efforts to kill us off, either literally or figuratively (i.e. "kill the Indian to save the man"). By linking our current reality to our shared history with non-First Nations people I am not attempting to make excuses for our reality; rather, I am simply offering context, and you can decide for yourself how to interpret the information or what to believe. First Nations people do not need anyone to feel sorry for us. What we need is for everyone, including First Nations people, to understand what our issues are, how they evolved, what our strengths are, what can be done to foster positive change, and how we all can contribute to that change. If you haven't been a part of the solution thus far, reading this book can be step one. Passing on the knowledge you gain is an easy way to help create sustainable positive change.

Whose version of history have you heard so far? History has been defined by those who wrote about it and had the means to distribute their version of history to the masses. First Nations people have been struggling for decades to bring forth the truth about our own pre-contact history, as well our shared history with non-First Nations people as we know it. This has been a long and arduous battle as there continues to be ongoing efforts to keep divergent points of view on history out of classrooms from kindergarten to university, and out of the halls of justice, libraries, films, and books. This gate keeping not only hurts First Nations people; it deprives all of us from knowing the truth about our shared history and its effects on all of our lives today. For First Nations people, revealing the truth is very important as we cannot just carry on as if nothing has happened. Counsellors and psychiatrists will agree that it is necessary to uncover the truth behind the symptoms of pain before true healing can happen. Without acknowledgement of our shared history and its effects on First Nations people, the road towards true reconciliation will be a long and bumpy one for all.

Most of the current issues for First Nations people stem from the colonization process. For over 500 years in the East and over 100 in the West, ongoing assimilation acts, policies, and laws have had very negative consequences for our communities. The *Canadian Constitution* and the *Indian Act* were both utilized to separate us from our land and place us on reserves, dismantle our governance structures, devalue women by imposing patriarchal laws, legally prohibit our cultural and spiritual practices, and relegate us to live in 'third world' conditions. Legislation was used to forcibly remove children from our communities to attend residential schools in order to make the assimilation process easier, and then to remove our children from our homes into foster care (which was essentially punishing us for the loss of parenting skills brought on through the residential school experience). Imposed laws continue to severely compromise the existence and strength of our traditional languages, allow others to steal our cultural objects and human remains, and utilize a foreign justice system to keep us separated from our children, lands, and resources. Historical records and books diminish our place in our homelands, disregard our creation stories directly linked to North America, devalue our culture and traditions, make us subjects of study for anthropologists and scientists, hide the truth about forced sterilization and other acts of genocide, and distort history to legitimize the forced colonization of North America. While all of these systematic attacks on our way of life has been devastating to our communities, the most devastating and far-reaching impacts stemmed from the Indian residential schools that were set up to 'educate' and assimilate First Nations people into mainstream society and Christianity. It has been publicly acknowledged by the Government of Canada and the churches that ran the schools that the policy was wrong and has resulted in ongoing devastating social effects for First Nations people. The irony is that their efforts to assimilate us resulted in our marginalization and many of the social issues that affect everyone in this country. You will read more about residential schools and many of its negative effects in the *Social Control* chapter.

Often you will hear non-First Nations people say, "that was a long time ago, why should it matter now;" "I didn't do it to them, so why should I care or pay;" or "why can't they just get over it?" These questions are based on a deep-rooted ignorance of our shared history and an individualized self-centered approach to living in a communal world and on traditional First Nations land. Although neither my mother nor I went to residential school, my children and I are profoundly impacted by the legacy of all the generations before us that were forced to attend. A few of the most evident ways that I continue to be negatively impacted are that I did not grow up in my traditional territories, did not even know my specific Nation until I was in my teens, did not have access to my Nation's songs and dances until I was in my thirties, and do not speak my ancestral language. My mother died at the age of 40 due to her addiction which helped her to cope with her pain; I dropped out of an alternate school and then struggled to learn parenting skills as a 16 year-old; and most of my immediate and extended family struggled at some point with their own demons. While these are some of the challenges that I've faced due to our history as First Nations people in Canada, I have also inherited an amazing strength and resiliency from my ancestors that has helped many, many generations of First Nations people survive assimilation policies and practices that have led to great challenges for themselves, their families, and their communities. Just knowing the amount of strength, conviction, and resiliency that it has taken for us as a people to survive gives me great strength and hope for the future.

Although economic, social, and political hardship is the reality for many First Nations people, I have complete faith that we are no different than any other people who face multiple challenges such as racism, poverty, and generational abuses. The primary difference for First Nations people is that an entire people were forced to suffer together, so we share the memories, shame, confusion and anger. In addition, there were very few First Nations people who were not negatively impacted by residential schools and therefore not many were capable of helping the masses to recover. I draw strength from our ancestors who survived these unthinkable atrocities and refused to completely give up our cultural teachings so that we could (re)learn them today, and from my children who give me hope for the future of our Nations as they are living proof that things can change drastically for the better in one generation.

Our recovery as a people will be heavily influenced by how well First Nations and non-First Nations people support the ongoing healing and development of First Nations youth as almost 60% of the First Nations community is under the age of 25. They are the fastest growing demographic in Canada, so this percentage will continue to rise. Along with this is the reality that almost 60% of all First Nations people now live in cities. There is little possibility that this trend will reverse in any considerable way without significant community and social development in First Nations communities. So if we are willing to work together to create positive change for us all, then these are the two groups that need immediate meaningful attention, resources, and support.

Now that you have a basic understanding of the underlying factors that have contributed to the many issues First Nations communities face today, I will not repeat these facts over and over again. Rather, you should keep them in mind when reading the rest of *First Nations 101* and think about how each subject relates back to these long-term influences. You can also take this one step further by thinking about how the healing and rebuilding of First Nations communities will positively affect the entire country economically and socially. *First Nations 101* ends with a few of the things that I believe must be accomplished in order for First Nations individuals, families and communities to fully recover from the long-lasting effects of assimilationist acts, laws, and policies. I am not an expert on all things related to First Nations people and do not have all the answers, but these are many practical suggestions that I believe can be implemented immediately to help make meaningful and long-lasting change.

How to use this book

In the tradition of my ancestors, *First Nations 101* is presented in a way that will tell you a story about First Nations people that stretches back to pre-contact. After a brief introduction to statistics and diversity, *Chapter 1* will introduce you to our ancestors. You will learn what life was like in First Nations communities before first contact with non-First Nations people. You will see us as you likely have never envisioned us before. I am not talking about the stereotypical stoic Indian who wandered the plains; rather, you will be introduced to a worldview that most, if not all, First Nations had in common. This will give you a basic understanding of why we refuse to let go of our cultures and traditions as they have such great meaning, teachings, and positive things to live our lives by today. These teachings and ways of life cannot be relegated to the past. In fact, we need them now more than ever.

Chapter 2 is an overview of our shared history in this country now known as Canada. I provide a broad overview of the many ways in which non-First Nations people and ensuing governments have imposed a form of social control over First Nations people through various actions, policies, and laws. This historical overview will paint a very clear picture of the systematic ways that our way of life was attacked, our lands and resources were taken, and history was distorted to whitewash the truth.

Chapter 3 provides a snapshot of the current realities for First Nations people. You will learn about the many social, political, cultural, and spiritual challenges that many of us face today. These issues are the direct result of the policies imposed upon us and the attitudes that non-First Nations people and governments have towards us to this very day. You will begin to understand the complexities of our day-to-day lives and how they are affected by the past few centuries of assimilation attempts that were described in *Chapter 2*.

In *Chapter 4,* I have tried to show that fairness and justice has been out of the reach of First Nations people for a very long time in the mainstream legal system and in the way that governments and other Canadians treat us. Publicly, there appears to be ways in which the Government of Canada is seeking to atone for its past sins against First Nations people, but when you take a closer look you will realize that it is all just window dressing. Hopefully, any shock or anger that may arise will move you towards action to help reverse this ongoing process that inhibits true justice for First Nations people.

In *Chapter 5,* I highlight some of the significant ways in which First Nations people are working towards true healing. The examples provided are efforts by First Nations people themselves, not something that has been imposed by government. We know what works for us; we just need governments to let us define our own future instead of continuing to impose their solutions upon us. This has very rarely worked in the past, and won't work now. I hope that the examples that I share about the diverse ways in which First Nations people are making a meaningful difference in their communities will inspire you to help contribute to their efforts.

Chapter 6 celebrates our will to thrive rather than simply survive. You will be introduced to the creativity that abounds in First Nations communities. These fabulous people are great examples of what a First Nations person can achieve if they have someone who believes in them and they have equal access to opportunities to learn and to express themselves. If nothing else, you'll have lots of new artists to add to your mp3 player, books to read, and videos to watch.

My greatest hope for *First Nations 101* is that it will change the way that First Nations people are thought of. In doing so, I hope that you will be moved to help create positive change for First Nations people through your own actions, both big and small. We can all learn from Francine Lemay whose brother was the only person to lose his life during the Oka Crisis of 1990. Years later, after learning the truth about the history of the Mohawk people, she found forgiveness and realized that it was a shared non-First Nations and First Nations history that led to the Oka events and loss of her brother. In 2010, Francine Lemay translated *At the Wood's Edge,* an anthology about the Mohawks of Kanesatake, into French for the 20th anniversary of the Oka Crisis so that more people would be exposed to the truth that led up to the crisis. In *Chapter 7, The Road Forward: Forging A New Path,* I provide practical things that all of us can do to foster positive change not only for First Nations people, but also for everyone else living in our traditional territories (all of North America). I truly believe that knowing the truth about our shared history and working together is the only way to make meaningful and long-lasting change, and to work towards reconciliation between First Nations and non-First Nations people. Please take the time to look at each of the lists to see what you can do or what you can help to force governments to do as we work together to create a new history that is based on truth, trust, partnership, and respect.

Find Out More

From Truth to Reconciliation: Transforming the Legacy of Residential Schools. M. Brant Castellano, L. Archibald and M. DeGagne. Aboriginal Healing Foundation. 2008.

Response, Responsibility, and Renewal: Canada's Truth and Reconciliation Journey. Aboriginal Healing Foundation. 2009.

Everything You Know About Indians Is Wrong. Paul Chatt Smith. University of Minnesota Press. 2009.

Anishnaabe World: A Guide for Building Bridges between Canada and First Nations. Roger Spielmann. 2009.

Stolen From Our Embrace: The Abduction of First Nations Children and the Restoration of Aboriginal Communities.

Suzanne Fournier and Ernie Crey. Douglas & McIntyre. 1998.
A Tortured People: The Politics of Colonization. Howard Adams. Theytus Books. 1995.
A Fair Country: Telling Truths About Canada. John Ralston Saul. Penguin Books. 2008.
A sister's grief bridges a cultural divide. Loreen Pindera. CBC News Online. July 8, 2010.

Not Just Numbers

First Nations people are over-represented in most negative statistics. We have high rates of diabetes, suicide, non-completion of high school, and homelessness. While this is not who we are, we are often looked at as statistics, which causes some people to expect those outcomes for us. This only exacerbates the problem as those who expect less of others tend to put forth less effort to help them rise above those expectations. This is played out every day in a school near you, in the justice system, and within social worker's offices across North America. While some of us are doing well, there are many others who still fall into these troubling statistics. Until those in positions of power begin to see us as more than a problem statistic, there can be no meaningful improvement for First Nations people.

While it is important to pay attention to statistical indicators of problem areas so that planning, initiatives, funding, and other resources can be put towards fostering positive change, we also need to pay attention to those statistics that show that some First Nations people are doing well, or at least better. For instance, while First Nations people suffer from depression and other mental health issues, we have very low incidence of organic mental health issues such as schizophrenia or bipolar disorder. A strength-based approach can be very enlightening for those who do not truly know us beyond what the statistics and stereotypes tell them. Once there is a meaningful effort put forth to understand our communities, issues, culture, and strengths, many are pleasantly surprised to realize that there is boundless untapped potential within us as both individuals and communities.

We as First Nations people also need to be aware of how statistics are used against us, or as an excuse to ignore us. Until statistics show politicians that we vote at a higher rate than the current 10% or less that we do, there will be no reason for them to pay attention to us or our needs. While I do understand the resistance to participate in the mainstream political system, I also see how our participation can lead to positive change for our communities. I believe that we must empower ourselves by any ethical means necessary in order to create positive change for future generations, as well as ourselves today.

Diversity: We Are Not All the Same

Despite popular opinion, First Nations people are not all the same. Most First Nations people share similar world views, but we have unique was of expressing our culture through songs, dance, art, kinship, and hierarchy. The region that a community inhabited had a great influence on their food, transportation methods, art, celebrations, and regalia. For instance, people from the Northwest Coast were amongst an abundance of food, so they had more time to develop their governance structure, art, celebrations and regalia, whereas people from northern areas had to spend larger amounts of time hunting and gathering food during warm weather to prepare for the long, cold winter months, so they had less time to establish elaborate governance structures, permanent housing, and art forms. These are some of the ways that we vary across Canada:

- *Aboriginal*: Canada's official name for the three distinct groups that are recognized within the *Canadian Constitution*: They are First Nations, Métis, and Inuit. It is important to note that the Inuit and Métis have very distinct histories, cultures, and relationship to governments, so many of the items below do not pertain to them as they are not governed by the *Indian Act.*

- *Status*: The Government of Canada only recognizes certain people as 'Status Indians' through the *Indian Act.* Therefore, there are both status and non-status individuals despite their blood quantum, residency, lineage, or recognition from their First Nations community. As a group, neither the Métis or Inuit people were ever given Indian status, but some may have gained status through marriage or parentage.

- *Indigenous Nations*: There are 45 unique Nations within the borders of Canada, plus the Inuit and Métis.

- *Bands*: Most Nations are made up of a number of Bands that each have their own Band Chief and Council, land, and community. There are 608 Bands in Canada.
- *Tribal Councils*: Some Nations form Tribal Councils of all or some of their individual Bands. These Councils usually work together on common issues.
- *Languages*: There are 23 unique languages across Canada (up to 50 when you count unique dialects). Fifteen of the larger language groups are in British Columbia, making it the most diverse language area in Canada.
- *Housing* was dictated in large part by the land. People of the Northwest Coast had warmer weather and giant cedar trees to build multi-family dwellings; people from the plains had to move around during the seasons so they needed easily transportable housing such as tipis; and the Inuit made igloos out of snow.
- *Clothing* was also influenced by the land. People in warmer climates did not need heavy clothing to survive the winters so they were able to use smaller pelts, woven garments, and bark to make functional clothing. On the other hand, people from colder climates needed much warmer and durable clothing due to the harsh winters and high mobility so their clothing would include heavy leather, fur, and lots of layers.
- *Social Structure*: First Nations communities vary in their social structure - from matrilineal and patrilineal; to matriarchs, clans mothers and Chiefs; to single family and multiple family dwellings; to hierarchical, which may include some families or individuals recognized as something akin to royalty.
- *Spirituality*: While First Nations people are traditionally spiritual people, the way that this was expressed varied

from Nation to Nation. For instance, sweatlodges are more from the plains, but people on the Northwest Coast had steam baths; sweetgrass is primarily found on the plains, while cedar boughs are found on the Northwest Coast; Sundances are practiced by people in hotter climates; sacred medicines varied from area to area; and everyone had medicine people and spiritual leaders.

- *Distinct Features*: If you look closely, you can see unique characteristics amongst people of various Nations. The most common traits are distinctive cheekbones, noses, height, body shape, and traditional hair styles.

- *Modern common beliefs and symbols*: Since the transmission of First Nations cultures was disrupted, many of us are only now learning about First Nations culture in any way that is available to us. So for those of us who are displaced from our traditional territories and cultural teachings, we are embracing teachings from other Nations that have evolved to become shared amongst many First Nations people. Things such as the medicine wheel, dream catchers, and the term Two-spirit (LGBT) have now been embraced by most First Nations people even though these beliefs may have originated from a Nation other than their own.

There are many other ways in which First Nations people are unique, but for the most part we have a common worldview which makes us more alike than different.

Chapter 1

Identity

This chapter provides a brief overview of what First Nations communities used to be like prior to first contact with non-First Nations people. This information is vital in understanding why the attempted forced full-scale assimilation of First Nations people is such a great injustice. As you will see, First Nations people had very distinct cultures that were based on the best interest of the community.

Overall, First Nations people were natural community developers: children were cherished and well-cared for; women, Elders and Two-spirit (LGBT) individuals were valued; each individual's strengths were identified and utilized for the benefit of the community; governance systems were strong and met the needs of the particular Nations and communities; and learning was a life-long process that everyone contributed to and benefitted from. As you will read in further chapters, it was the forced assimilation of First Nations people over several hundred years that directly led to the disintegration of our communities and our current social and economic reality.

Culture

Culture is an expression of a worldview which in turn is the core of a person's identity. Since the beginning of time First Nations people have had very distinct and unique cultures. Overall, most First Nations, regardless of where they were located, had a connection to and respect for the earth, were communal in nature, practiced sacred spiritual ceremonies, and were oral-based peoples who passed on our history through storytelling, pictographs, art, songs, and dances. While dancing, regalia, food and many other things are an important expression of culture, they are not culture itself.

Culture provides people with a sense of belonging, a connection to their Creator and each other, and a feeling that they are a part of something bigger than their individual selves. Culture provides a communal bond and common understanding of our roles within a community and the world. The expression of culture through song, dance, clothing, and ceremonies may have differed due to such things as geography, which included various animals living in the region that were used for regalia and as clan symbols, or the weather patterns that could limit activity. Many First Nations songs and dances tell a story or honor the world around us. My Nation, Tsimshian, has songs and dances that honor our four clans as they were incredibly important in the structure and everyday functioning of our communities. Plains First Nations have the chicken dance and crow hop, and the Apaches have the eagle dance. Some Nations have secret societies that only practice their songs and dances in a closed setting, in specific settings, and in the presence of select people. The ownership of songs and dances varied from Nation to Nation. On the Northwest Coast most songs and dances were owned by an individual or family. No one else could use or practice them unless they had permission. When someone was given the right to use a song or dance there was usually a public announcement and sometimes an exchange of something else for that right. Other Nations did things differently – some of their songs were communally owned and shared openly.

First Nations culture was centred on spirituality. This was evident through most everything we did in our daily lives. We were a prayerful people, practiced many sacred ceremonies, and had a strong connection to the land, each other, our families, communities, and our ancestors. Prayer and giving thanks to the Creator and to living beings that had given up their lives so that we could eat or clothe ourselves was a normal part of our everyday lives. We understood that life itself was a gift from the Creator, so we must value it. We also understood that the Creator provided for us in many ways so that we could live and fulfill our responsibilities as human beings. That is true culture. It defined us, inspired us, made us accountable, gave us purpose, ensured we were thankful, and ensured that we were mindful as we knew that our actions could either positively or negatively affect the next seven generations to come.

Find Out More

And Grandma Said: Iroquois teachings as passed down through the oral tradition. Tom Porter. Xlibris Corporation. 2008.
First Nations Confederacy of Cultural Education Centres

Ceremonies

Ceremonies were an integral part of First Nations people's daily lives. We had countless ceremonies and rituals serving distinct purposes that brought the community together in times of sorrow, prayer, transition, and celebration. Some ceremonies were purely spiritual in nature, while others publically marked milestones for individuals, families, or the community. Specific ceremonies were held for significant events such as the birth of a child, raising a totem pole, in times of transition like puberty, marriage, and death, and the transfer of Chieftainships, names, songs, or dances.

Ceremonies passed from generation to generation, were given to us in dreams or ceremony, or were developed when the need arose. Ceremonies could range from a single prayer or action to elaborate multi-day experiences which involved as few as one or two people to as many as an entire community. They were carried out in both public and private locations that were identified or created for those specific purposes. Ceremonies were led by individuals who had been trained from an early age after they were identified as being born into the role or were identified as having been uniquely gifted with specific knowledge and skills.

Traditional medicines were a large part of ceremonies. Our medicines not only helped us to fight physical health problems, they also helped us to connect to the Creator and to purify, protect, and heal ourselves spiritually, emotionally, and mentally. Medicines used to prevent or heal illness were found all around us in our traditional territories and beyond. If they were not indigenous to our territory, we might have traded with other First Nations people to acquire it. Some of our medicines included sage, sweetgrass, tobacco, and cedar. We believe that the burning of these medicines help to cleanse us, heal us, and take our prayers to the Creator.

The eagle is one of the things to which you can find a common connection amongst most First Nations across North

America. Since the eagle is so sacred and well respected, many parts of its body are used in ceremony or as a sacred part of regalia. Eagles are often represented through clans, houses, or totems. The eagle is considered very sacred due to its closeness to the Creator, commitment to family, and its prevalence in many prophecies.

All First Nations communities had rights of passage to help individuals transition into new phases and responsibilities in their lives. These formal ceremonies included witnesses who supported and encouraged the individual. These ceremonies helped an individual to understand their rights and responsibilities in their new role. The ceremony was followed by a period of teaching and mentoring that modelled the proper skills and behaviors. One of the most important transition times was when young people went through puberty and became young women and men. During this time they were educated about what was happening with them physically and spiritually and what their new responsibilities and rights were so that they could work toward becoming a responsible adult.

Find Out More

God Is Red. Vine Deloria Jr. Fulcrum Publishing. 1994.
Peace, Power, Righteousness: An Indigenous Manifesto, 2nd Edition. Taiaiake Alfred. Oxford University Press. 2009.
White Buffalo Teachings. Arvol Lookinghorse. Dreamkeepers Press. 2001.

Check Your Head – Spirituality & Religion

Contrary to the widespread belief of North America's first immigrants, we were not pagans or atheists. All First Nations people believed in and gave thanks to a Creator in some form. The key difference between our worshipping practices and most non-First Nations practices is the formality of how it was promoted and expressed in general. Traditional First Nations practice is more accurately described as spirituality rather than religion as the main emphasis was on the spiritual connection with the Creator. It was not based on hierarchies, blame, shame, or male dominance. Rather, it was based on building and maintaining our spiritual selves and fulfilling our responsibilities as beings on this earth by being connected to and caring for the land, each other, our ancestors, other living beings such as animals and plants, and the Creator in our daily lives. While there were longhouses, sweatlodges, and tipis where ceremony could be carried out at specific times and for specific purposes, for the most part we carried our beliefs with us at all times and practiced our spiritual beliefs when we wanted or needed to wherever we were.

Potlatches

Since time immemorial, First Nations people have hosted formal cultural ceremonies to mark significant events in the community. For people of the Northwest Coast of North America we hosted potlatches. Things that were recognized and/or celebrated included births, marriages, deaths, totem pole raising, giving of traditional names, and passing on names, songs, dances, or other cultural responsibilities. These things were carried out publicly to be inclusive of the community and to have witnesses who could verify what work was done and that it was done properly by following cultural protocols. The potlatch, along with other First Nations ceremonies, was legally banned from 1884 to 1951 in order to help the government forcibly assimilate us into mainstream society. Despite this ban, many of our ancestors still potlatched in secrecy. Their devotion to keeping this tradition alive led to many being jailed, most notably during Dan Cranmer's 1921 potlatch which resulted in almost 50 people being arrested. Over half were jailed, others were forced to give up their regalia, and all of the masks, rattles, and other cultural items were confiscated. The Kwakwaka'wakw fought for decades to recover most of the 200 items that they have been able to identify; however, no one is sure how many more were taken. Fortunately, there were pictures taken before the items were shipped off to the Canadian Museum of Civilization, the Royal Ontario Museum, and to private collectors; these pictures were instrumental in helping to prove that the items belonged to the Kwakwaka'wakw people. Most of these items are now housed in the U'mista Cultural Centre in Alert Bay, B.C. Today, the potlatch is alive and well in some communities, but most still struggle to relearn the songs, dances, and protocols that were forgotten due to the prohibition.

Contrary to popular Euro-centric belief, potlatches were not the economic engine for the community. Traditional Northwest Coast communities were not built upon European ideas of economic prosperity; rather, they were built upon community prosperity based primarily on our individual, cultural, and social and spiritual well-being. The potlatch is a means of practicing and uplifting our cultural and spiritual protocols and beliefs, not a display or distribution of material wealth. Of course, today some individuals may have adopted an economic view of the potlatch, but that is not its true essence or purpose. The distribution of resources was secondary to the cultural, social, and spiritual significance of the potlatch. The gift of a woven chilkat robe or a canoe was not based on its monetary value, but rather its cultural value which was considered more important and even prestigious. Cultural protocols ensure that the spiritual and cultural beliefs of the community are adhered to and are preserved for the generations that follow.

Since the Northwest Coast was so bountiful with food and resources, we did not have to spend vast amounts of our time trying to find and preserve food. Once we had enough food to last through the winter it was possible for us to potlatch for up to a few weeks at a time. In today's modern world, potlatches usually last only one or two days. Many people contributed to the potlatch by preparing food for the guests, making goods or food to give as gifts to Chiefs, Elders, or other guests. Depending on what the potlatch was being held to commemorate, who was in attendance, and who was hosting it, gifts could be as generous as carved masks, canoes, woven blankets, copper shields, or oolichan grease. One cannot under-estimate the amount of time, resources, and energy it takes to host a traditional potlatch; it usually takes years to plan and prepare for. There are many significant areas to work on including cooking and serving entire meals to hundreds of guests, organizing singers and dancers to fill all of the time, tending the fire, gathering, making and distributing gifts, being the behind-the-scenes floor manager who ensures people are ready to enter at the right time, and being the person who speaks on behalf of the host. These are just some of the countless responsibilities that must be fulfilled before, during, and after a potlatch to ensure a potlatch runs smoothly.

Find Out More

Box of Treasures. Video by Chuck Olin and U'mista Cultural Centre. 1983.

The Potlatch Collection. U'mista Cultural Society. Alert Bay, British Columbia.

Potlatch: A Strict Law Bids Us Dance (DVD). Dennis Wheeler. U'mista Cultural Society. 1975.

Governance

Since time immemorial, First Nations people had governance structures that ensured that everyone in the community was taken care of; the best interest of the community or Nation was the primary goal. 'Egalitarian' is the term anthropologists like to use. Of course, there were what some might call hierarchies and most Nations had Chiefs or someone with similar responsibilities, but there were also systems such as the potlatch that ensured that there was an ongoing distribution of resources so that the whole community prospered. The most common governance systems included clans, houses, confederacies, and councils.

First Nations each had their own unique way of governing their communities and Nations. There are geographical and historic reasons that have contributed to how Nations functioned and what they were or were not able to spend large amounts of time developing and maintaining, including complex governance systems. People who had to travel frequently to different sites to find food and/or shelter usually had less complex social and governance structures. These communities would be more focused on families and smaller groups of people rather than complex social structures of large communities like those found on the Northwest Coast of B.C. For instance, I am a member of the Tsimshian Nation which includes houses, clans, crests, Matriarchs, and hereditary Chiefs. In addition, my Nation is matriarchal, so my children follow my lineage and clan. My children's father is Cree. His community has what would be equivalent to a clan or crest, but no houses. His Nation is patrilineal, so my children should follow his lineage and clan as well. There are far too many variations across North America to list, so here are a few simple explanations for your reference.

Clans – In my Nation, we have four clans into which everyone belongs to one. Each clan usually represents an animal which is significant in the area and to our people. Our clans are the Eagle, Raven, Killer Whale, and Wolf. I was born into the

Killer Whale Clan through my mother. In essence, a Clan is like an extended family as each member is considered related to each other. When there is a significant event in the community, such as a death, each clan has specific responsibilities to uphold in relation to things that must take place regarding that person's death.

Houses – Some Nations are grouped into houses, with each house including other houses or groupings of people/ families within them. Each house has its own Chief, and each person is born into a house. The easiest general comparison is that of the National Hockey League which has several divisions with many teams within each one.

The Iroquois Confederacy (also known as the Six Nations) include the Cayuga, Oneida, Onondaga, Mohawk, Seneca, and Tuscarora Nations. Each of these Nations was Haudenosaunee or People of the Longhouse. Each Nation adhered to the Great Law of Peace as they worked together as a Grand Council on issues of common importance in maintaining their traditional way of life and warding off enemies as Europeans began to populate North America. Each Nation was free to make autonomous decisions relating to their own Tribe's internal matters. This democratic system was said to have influenced the creation of the United States Constitution. However, it seems that one very important part of Iroquois Confederacy governance system was ignored in the U.S. Constitution: the involvement of Clan Mothers who could appoint a Chief or take away his authority if he was not acting in the best interest of the people.

Find Out More

Governance Best Practices Report. National Centre for First Nations Governance. 2009.

Native Nations Institute for Leadership, Management, and Policy.

Everyone has a Place in the Circle

Traditional First Nations communities were inclusive, not exclusive. Everyone had a place in the community despite their gender, physical or mental ability, sexual orientation, or age. Women, Elders, Two-spirit, children, and youth were an integral part of a healthy and vibrant community. While some people were born into certain roles such as a hereditary Chief, each person's unique circumstances were usually tapped into for the best interest of the community. Their roles could be influenced by their age, gender, physical or mental ability, and their unique gifts in areas such as art, spirituality, hunting, storytelling, or leadership. Each person's tasks and gifts were complimentary to everyone else's and contributed to the ongoing development and maintenance of the community.

> *"As children we are encouraged to discover and master the special gifts planted inside us by the creator and through our ancestors. These gifts are intentional and important to offer, as adults, in the Tribal Circle."*
>
> Ramona Peters, Mashpee Wampanoag

Young children usually did not have specific roles that they had to fulfill; rather, their task was to learn from older generations so that the community could ensure the transmission of traditional knowledge and practices to future generations. As children grew and their gifts were identified, they would begin their more formal learning through observation, listening, participation, and practice. Youth took on new responsibilities as they learned more and could contribute on a daily basis to the overall functioning of the community. Where gendered roles existed, youth would find their place and learn from adults through instruction, observation, and hands-on learning as they moved towards increased levels of responsibility within their family and community.

Adults, as the middle group, were responsible for raising children and youth as well as supporting Elders, their families, and communities. Depending on the Nation and community, women took on many different roles within the community including as hunters, cooks, medicine people, mediators, and Matriarchs. Men's dominance had not yet been introduced through contact with non-First Nations people. Rather, women and men often shared and had complimentary roles that depended on each other's cooperation, respect, and assistance. This reciprocal and supportive way of being ensured that everyone contributed to and benefited from the community's health and prosperity.

In most First Nations communities Two-spirit people (lesbian, gay, bi-sexual, and transgender) were acknowledged and honored with specific roles in their community. You can find out more in the next section 'Two-spirit – LGBT'.

Elders had a unique, special, and irreplaceable role within our communities. The term 'Elder' is not a traditional name that First Nations used; rather, there were specific names for older and wiser people in each language. Those terms acknowledged the unique and special role that individuals held in our communities as culture bearers, holders of great wisdom, teachers, and many other important things that kept our communities and cultures alive and thriving. I do not know where the term 'Elder' comes from, but its origin is likely similar to the term 'Two-spirit'; both are words that can be used universally to fit the modern way of labelling something so it can fit into mainstream reality which views First Nations people from a pan-First Nations perspective, lumping all Nations together into one homogenous group.

People who had physical or other limitations were not disregarded; rather, their role was adjusted so that they could be a part of and contribute to the community.

Find Out More

Restoring the Balance: First Nations Women, Community, and Culture. E. Guimond, G.G. Valaskakis and Madeleine Dion Stout, editors. University of Manitoba Press. 2009.

Two Spirit Women 2nd Edition. Doris O'Brien-Teengs. 2-Spirited People of the 1st Nations. 2008.
Two Spirit People: American Indian Lesbian Women and Gay Men. Lester B. Brown. Routledge. 1997.

Two-spirit – LGBT

There are few people today who know the rich history of lesbian, gay, bisexual, and transgender (Two-spirit) people within First Nations communities. Traditionally, First Nations people valued and had a place for everyone in the community including Two-spirit people. In contrast to mainstream society, First Nations people did not view being Two-spirit as being primarily about one's sexuality. Rather, Two-spirit people were thought to embody both feminine and masculine spirits and qualities and were viewed as being spiritually attuned. Many First Nations people now refer to First Nations LGBT individuals as Two-spirit, a term that was coined by First Nations academics in the 1980s as a way of acknowledging the unique beliefs of First Nations regarding genders other than strictly male and female.

In his book *Changing Ones: Third and Fourth Genders in Native North America*, Will Roscoe provides a good overview of Two-spirit traditions within First Nations communities. He highlights beliefs of various Nations, includes historical pictures of Two-spirit individuals dressed in what would be considered their opposite gender style, and lists specific Indigenous names for Two-spirit people within distinct Nations across North America including the Tlingit word 'gatxan' meaning halfman-halfwoman, the Inuit word 'sipiniq' meaning infant whose sex changes at birth, the Blackfoot word 'ake:skassi' meaning acts like a woman, the Tsimshian word 'kana'ts', Apache word 'n desdzan' meaning man-woman, and the Hopi word 'kwasaitaka' meaning skirt man. Since Two-spirit people were thought to embody both male and female spirits, they were believed to be able to more easily relate to both males and females, so they often played the role of mediator. They were also seen as being very much in touch with their spiritual side, so were given roles of honor including wrapping of the center pole for sundances, being medicine people, and leading ceremonies. Some individuals also took on the role of the opposite gender such as hunting, cooking, child rearing, or other gender-specific roles which might also include dressing in the way that accompanied that gender or gender role such as hunting outfits.

Despite the healthy and honorable First Nations history in relation to Two-spirit people, there are now various levels of homophobia among First Nations individuals, families, and communities. This change was brought about through the introduction of Euro-centric religious-based beliefs that devalued LGBT people. This reality led to the organization of the National Aboriginal LGBTQT Summit in Vancouver in 2008 which saw Two-spirit individuals, Elders, funders, government representatives, policy makers, and family members come together to find ways to better support Two-spirit people. Most participants felt that the seismic shift in beliefs from acceptance and honor to exclusion and shame has led to many Two-spirit people suffering from abuse, being shamed and disowned, having low self-esteem and suicidal ideation, and struggling with many unhealthy coping mechanisms. Many Two-spirit individuals are often shunned by their families and/or communities so they are forced to flee for their own physical or emotional safety. Many are also blocked from participating in community-based cultural practices and ceremonies. Often when Two-spirit people move to cities they face racism, poverty, and isolation. Many non-First Nations people assume that the traditional teachings and values regarding Two-spirit people are still being practiced today. This often leads to the mistaken belief that Two-spirit people are revered and taken care of in our communities, when in reality that is rarely the case. This confusion results in many Two-spirit individuals being left with very little to no social support or acknowledgement that they may have unique needs as a Two-spirit person. Parents at the LGBTQT Summit advocated for more cultural teachings and support for themselves and their Two-spirit child. They shared that many family members feel very confused, isolated, scared, and lacking in knowledge of where to go for help so that they can better understand the dynamics involved with their child coming out and how to support their child.

At a time when First Nations people are working towards healing and regaining their traditional beliefs and practices, we could definitely use all the help we can get. It is painfully ironic that although traditionally Two-spirit people were often in roles that helped to solve problems and helped people heal, today they are often denied the right to take their rightful place in our communities even if it means that we are rejecting individuals who could help us to more quickly recover as families and communities. Despite the current challenges, growing numbers of people are learning about and embracing traditional Two-spirit beliefs, including family members who work to re-educate others so that their loved ones can be safely welcomed back into their families and communities. The largest celebration and ongoing support of Two-spirit history can be found at the International Two-spirit Gatherings that have been held across North America for more than 20 years. This annual gathering is a safe place for Two-spirit people and their partners, Elders, and other supporters to network, celebrate, carry out spiritual practices, organize, and plan outreach work to help revive the proud Two-spirit history and beliefs. Many support groups are forming, including one or two First Nations PFLAGs. Two-spirit people and their supporters are also developing resources such as websites and films as a way to help people to learn more about Two-spirit people and bring back traditional teachings and practices.

<u>Find Out More</u>

Changing Ones: Third and Fourth Genders in Native North America. Will Roscoe. Palgrave MacMillan. 1998.
2-Spirited People of the 1st Nations Society
Two Spirits: Belonging video. Rope Wolf. 2009.
International Two Spirit Gathering
Deb-we-win Ge-kend-am-aan, Our Place in the Circle video. Lorne Olson. 2008.
Transforming Generations: 15th Annual Two-spirit Gathering. 2-Spirited People of the 1st Nations. 2003.

Traditional Teachings / Education

Education in First Nations communities was a life-long process that included everyone in the community and was an integral part of our cultural practices and daily lives. Everyone was taught how to fulfill their roles in the community as children, youth, adults, and Elders. Everyone was learning from the day they were born until their last day. Each individual was responsible for passing on knowledge everyday in both formal and informal settings while cooking, hunting, carving, weaving, storytelling, or leading a ceremony.

First Nations forms of educating individuals were very different than systems that were introduced by Europeans, which had children learning outside of their family and immediate community while attending a school at specified times. Although informal, our systems of passing on knowledge were at the same time very structured and included defined roles when needed. From the time a child was born, they were learning. Babies were often carried on their mother's back in a position that allowed for them to see what was happening and to learn at all times. Parents included children in most community activities so that they could learn and benefit from simply being present and observing or participating and asking questions when appropriate. Our education was based on teaching everyone what they needed to know in order to help the community thrive economically, culturally, politically, and socially. This was in stark contrast to European systems that trained children to adjust and contribute to material wealth-based economies.

The foundation of First Nations history and culture is our oral traditions. Speech and storytelling was our primary teaching method and ensured that our histories and cultural ways were known and remembered throughout the generations. While history was also acknowledged and maintained through pictographs, art, songs, dances, and ceremonies, the primary way of recording our histories was orally. First Nations people were able to meaningfully and articulately recount our histories in any area of North America. The repeated recounting and sharing of stories ensured that the integrity of the information was not lost. Everyone made a conscious effort to share information from hands-on teaching to Elders utilizing storytelling.

Find Out More

Indigenous Storywork: Educating the Heart, Mind, Body, and Spirit. Jo-ann Archibald. UBC Press. 2009.

Sacred Ways of Life: Traditional Knowledge. National Aboriginal Health Organization. 2005.

And Grandma Said: Iroquois teachings as passed down through the oral tradition. Tom Porter. Xlibris Corporation. 2008.

Inuit

Inuit people are one of three distinct groups that are referred to as Aboriginal people in the *Canadian Constitution.* Inuit Tapiriit Kanatami (ITK), the national organization that represents the needs of Inuit people, reports that Inuit people have only been in Canada for 5,000+ years. The 2006 Canadian Census reported that there were 50,485 Inuit, which is 4.3% of the overall Aboriginal population. Fifty-six percent of Inuit are under the age of 25 which is a higher percentage than for all people in Canada including First Nations and Métis. Forty thousand (78%) of all Inuit live in four main areas that span from the Northwest Territories to Labrador which they call Inuit Nunaat which means 'Inuit Homeland' in Inuktitut, the main Inuit language. Inuit Nunaat includes Nunavut (24,635 or 49%), Inuvialuit in the Northwest Territories (3,115 or 6%), Nunavik in northern Quebec (9,565 or 19%), and Nunatsiavut in northern Labrador (2,160 or 4%). Inuit are the majority population in these areas (84% in Nunavut, 90% of Nunavik, 55% in Inuvialuit, 89% in Nunatsiavut). Seventeen percent (8,395) of all Inuit live in urban centres with the largest populations living in Ottawa/Gatineau (725), Yellowknife (640), Edmonton (590), Montréal (570), and Winnipeg (355). Another 5% live in rural areas outside Inuit Nunaat.

Officially recognized Inuit territories were created over a 30 year span through various agreements. The areas include 660,000 square kilometer Nunavik through the 1975 James Bay and Northern Quebec Agreement, 90,650 square kilometer Inuvialuit through the 1984 Inuvialuit Final Agreement, 2 million square kilometer Nunavut through the 1993 Nunavut Land Claims Agreement, and 72,500 square kilometer Nunatsiavut through the 2005 Labrador Inuit Land Claim Agreement. Most of the 52 communities within these regions can only be accessed by plane year-round or by boat in the summer months and have relatively low populations with 38% having less than 500 people, 29% having 500-999 people, and 33% having over 1,000 people.

Living in these remote northern territories presents very unique circumstances and issues that most other North Americans do not experience. The ITK and the Government of Nunavut continue to lobby the Government of Canada to recognize that the Inuit have very distinct concerns from that of the rest of Canada as well as from First Nations and Métis people.

The first issue is Inuit long-term occupation of the north which has helped to ensure Arctic sovereignty for Canada. The 2010 federal apology to Inuit people that were forced to relocate to the High Arctic has many speculating that the relocation was part of a plan to assert Canadian sovereignty in the area – an assertion that the Government of Canada denies. The relocation of 87 Inuit from their livable environment to the northern Arctic left them struggling to adapt to constant darkness in the winter and weather that was 20 degrees celsius colder, all while living in basic tents with little food to hunt across the rough terrain. Despite this shameful period, Inuit leaders are currently open to working with the federal government to help maintain Arctic sovereignty as well as their traditional way of life.

The Inuit have always hunted whales, seals, and other marine mammals to help sustain their families. Since the world started paying attention to the barbaric way that international seal hunters club baby seals to death in order to get their pelts for the valuable fur trade market, the Inuit have had to defend their traditional use of seals for not only food, but for clothing, oil, and other purposes. The Inuit are working to educate the average person and international governments about the Inuit inherent right to hunt seal. Three such actions in 2009 made a significant impact. They include having the Governor General of Canada eat seal meat in front of the media, the Okalakatiget Society producing the video called *A Traditional Seal Hunt in Nunatsiavut*, and Canadian and Greenland Inuit fighting against the European Parliament's proposed Seal Ban Regulation which would prohibit the import of seal fur into any European Union country. These actions and the advocacy of the Government of Canada will hopefully result in changing the mistaken view of the international community about Inuit hunting and use of seal.

The other internationally caused problem for the Inuit is global warming. Inuit are the first to see the devastating effects of global warming as some of their homes literally fall into the ocean when their land of ice melts away. While they used to be able to travel for days on end with their dog teams, by snowshoe, or by skidoo, this is now limited as chunks of ice break off and float off into the sea. The video of a young man stranded on one such chunk of land ice went viral in 2009. There are many people who are worried about the polar bear as the ice disappears, but we must also acknowledge and appreciate that global warming is not only forcing Inuit to rebuild and relocate, it is also forcing changes to their traditional way of life which includes hunting and fishing. It amazes me how humans can adapt to their environment and make it livable. Although many of us might think of their territories as harsh and difficult to live in, the Inuit appreciate it for its great beauty and uniqueness. They have demonstrated great ingenuity to survive in such challenging climate with the use of snow shoes, dog sleds, and their greatest engineering feat, the igloo. In an effort to maintain their inherent rights and traditional way of life, the Inuit are working to influence and improve Arctic policy in areas such as Inuit sovereignty, climate change, and resource development. Inuit Tapiriit Kanatami is developing Inuit Qaujisarvingat, a knowledge centre in Ottawa, which will help bridge the gap between Inuit knowledge and western science by working with governments and researchers and offering education and training in areas such as research, ethics guidelines, and the sharing of knowledge.

While many of us appreciate the Inuit for their culture, we choose to show it in a respectful way. Others do not. The Edmonton 'Eskimos' football team continues to use a name which the Inuit themselves do not use and many have said is offensive. Common respect leads me to call the Inuit people what they tell us their name is, not what others continue to perpetuate. The majestic Inukshuk also comes from the Inuit people, but few understand its true purpose and use. Non-Inuit people believe that the Inukshuk is used only to help those traveling long distances to find their way; however, it is used for many other purposes as is explained in *Tukiliit: The Stone People Who Live In The Wind*. The shape that is most commonly known is only one of the many Inuksuit that take many shapes and serve many purposes. It looks somewhat like the logo that the 2010 Olympic Committee displayed, but the logo is no match to the original. Unfortunately, Inuit representatives were not consulted before the Inukshuk was appropriated for the Winter Olympic in Vancouver, nor was it an Inuit person who submitted the design. Despite the circumstances, the Inuit used the opportunity to teach the world about the true meaning of Inukshuk and the history of their people. Lucky for the 2010 Olympic Committee!

Nunavut

On April 1, 1999, Nunavut officially took its place as Canada's newest territory after many years of land claims negotiations between the Inuit and the Government of Canada. Nunavut means 'Our Land' in the Inuktitut language. The 2,000,000 square kilometers of land in the eastern half of the former Northwest Territories makes up about 25% of Canada's land mass. Approximately 85% of the almost 30,000 residents are Inuit. The 26 communities range in population size from 25 to 6,000, with the largest being Iqaluit.

Nunavut presents a unique opportunity for Inuit people to be self-governing within their traditional territories. This brings with it many challenges in educating, training, and recruiting qualified Inuit candidates. The Nunavut government has partnered with a number of southern universities to help train Inuit people to become qualified for the government jobs within the mandated time. However, this is a long process and many jobs remain unfilled by Inuit in the meantime. Further benefits come from the concerted effort to ensure that Inuit culture and history are included in school curriculums and in written government documents.

The public government structure of Nunavut is unique in many ways including how Members of the Legislative Assembly (MLAs) are elected, how the Premier is selected, and their decision making process. MLAs are elected on an individual, rather than party basis. The Premier is then selected by the elected MLAs. Nunavut is run by a Consensus Government which means it is must have a majority to gain authority, but there is a clear effort to work together to achieve the goals that were identified during the election period. The consensus model is known as the Bathurst Mandate or Pinasuaqtavut which means "that which we set out to do". According to the Nunavut Government website, "the Bathurst Mandate is the statement of values and priorities that guides the conduct of government and identifies the common objectives of Members. It was completed in August 1999, and outlined guiding principles for the next five years. It defines specific objectives and sets out a vision of what Nunavut will look like in the future".

Find Out More

5,000 Years of Inuit History and Heritage. Inuit Tapiriit Kanatami. 2008.
Inuit Qaujisarvingat: The Inuit Knowledge Centre at ITK.
Tukiliit: The Stone People Who Live In The Wind. Norman Hallendy. Douglas & McIntyre. 2009.
Inuksuit: Silent Messengers of the Arctic. N. Hallendy. Douglas & McIntyre. 2001.
The Work of Angayuqaq Oscar Kawagley. J. Archibald, R. Barnhardt, G.A. Cajete, P. Cochran, E. McKinley and L. Merculieff. Cultural Studies of Science Education. Vol. 2, No. 1, January, 2007. Springer Netherlands.
The Experimental Eskimos video. Barry Greenwald. 2009.
A Traditional Seal Hunt In Nunatsiavut video. Okalakatiget Society. 2009.

Métis

The Métis are one of the three groups that are identified as Aboriginal people in the *Canadian Constitution*. The 2006 Canadian Census reports that there are 389,785 Métis (33.2% of the overall Aboriginal population). According to the Métis National Council (MNC), the Métis Nation has "a shared history, common culture (song, dance, dress, national symbols, etc.), unique language (Michif with various regional dialects), extensive kinship connections from Ontario westward, distinct way of life, traditional territory and collective consciousness." There are a growing number of resources dedicated to providing a historical record that incorporates Métis experience and knowledge.

The Métis originated in the mid-1800s in the Red River district of what is now known as Manitoba. This area was populated by many Europeans and First Nations people who were involved in the fur trade. Their close proximity and the perceived need to forge partnerships between First Nations and non-First Nations people resulted in many mixed marriages between First Nations women and French or Scottish men. The first people known as Métis were the children of these unions. The first official recognition of the Métis can be found in the 1870 *Manitoba Act* which provided for compensation to Métis people for the extinguishment of their rights and land title that they had as the descendants of First Nations people (through the issuance of a certificate known as 'scrip'). The government believed that the European fathers of the Métis children would financially support them and that those children would be assimilated into mainstream society. Section 81 of the *Act* set aside 1,400,000 acres of land to be divided amongst Métis individuals rather than being reserved as a collective land base as had been done previously with First Nations people through treaties – a decision that would have long-term negative consequence for the Métis as a Nation and as individuals. Each Métis head of a household was allotted 160 acres and each child 240 acres. The first allotment of land was finally distributed to just over 5,000 people six years later – a number that the Métis assert was only a portion of the individuals who were eligible to receive compensation. In the years following, the amount of land that was thought to be in Métis possession would greatly decrease through many ways including non-Métis speculators buying up or fraudulently obtaining land then reselling it, appropriation for government use or for immigrant settlement, and Métis individuals selling land as it was not farmable, to be closer to their family, or to obtain much needed money to survive. Métis organizations and researchers believe that almost 90% of Métis land was lost in these ways.

The MNC and its provincial counterparts have struggled for decades to have Métis rights and land title restored as a matter of justice and to allow them to have an official homeland from which to build their community and maintain their cultural traditions. The Province of Alberta is the only Canadian province or territory that has established a common land base for Métis known as Métis Settlements, of which there are currently seven. These settlements began in the late 1930s and have evolved to provide the Métis with limited self-government and resource rights. Constitutional recognition has helped the Métis to win some of their fishing and hunting rights through significant cases such as the 2003 *Powley* decision of the Supreme Court of Canada. Despite the federal government's assertion that all Métis rights were extinguished through the 1870 *Manitoba Act*, the Métis continue to assert land claims based on their inherent rights, the imposition of the *Act* upon them, and the way that the ensuing land distribution through scrip was mishandled. In the meantime, the MNC is working towards establishing how many Métis there are in Canada.

Currently, there is much contention across the country regarding who is and who is not Métis, especially as it relates to constitutional rights and some public benefits such as health insurance. Today there are First Nations individuals who are either non-status or have First Nations and other ancestry (aka mixed-blood) stating that they are Métis, when in fact they are not a descendant of a Métis person. Some refer to those who are direct descedants of those from the Red River area as 'big M' Métis, and all others as 'little m' Métis. The ongoing advocacy for Métis rights and land claims is putting pressure on Métis organizations to better define their membership criteria so that they can provide clear numbers of how many members they represent and to inform their land claims. Noted lawyer Jean Teillet provides a good overview of the legal intricacies of who can and cannot be defined as Métis in one or more contexts in the annually produced *Métis Law Summary*. She notes that the *Powley* decision differentiates between mere membership in an Aboriginal organization and genuine identification and life as a part of the Métis community or culture. The Métis National Council is working towards establishing a Métis Nation Registry that will include individuals who meet the MNC definition as "a person who self-identifies as Métis, is of historic Métis Nation Ancestry, is distinct from other Aboriginal Peoples and is accepted by the Métis Nation."

To mark the 125th anniversary of the Northwest Resistance and the execution of Louis Riel, who was a primary leader of the Métis people, the MNC declared 2010 to be the Year of the Métis as a platform from which to raise awareness about the Métis Nation.

Find Out More

The Métis Nation Magazine. Métis National Council.
Métis Land Rights and Self-Government. Leah Dorion, with Darren R. Préfontaine. Gabriel Dumont Institute. 2003.
Métis Law Summary. Jean Teillet. Pape Salter Teillet. 2009.
Métis National Council: Office of the President Newsletter
Louis Riel Institute
Back to Batoche Interactive Website
Pemmican Publications

Chapter 2
Social Control

My life and every other First Nations person's life has been greatly impacted by the many laws, policies, and actions that have been externally imposed upon us since first contact. Although many of these laws and policies were enacted generations ago, they are still having a profound effect on First Nations people as they have fundamentally changed the way our communities function, dispossessed us of our land, introduced unhealthy behaviors over many generations, and severely eroded many of our traditional cultural practices and languages. We continue to struggle to assert our autonomy as the first people of North America, recover from the physical, sexual, emotional, mental, and spiritual abuses that survivors experienced in the residential schools, fight in foreign-imposed justice systems to regain our lands, resources, and inherent right to govern ourselves, struggle within and outside of our communities to restore women, Elders, and Two-spirit people back into their traditionally honored places in our communities, and fight against the current colonial imposition of laws and policies such as the current *First Nations Governance Act*. These are just a few of the broad ways in which we are severely impacted in our daily lives by other people's actions. There are many, many more forms of social control that First Nations individuals face every day of our lives.

To look back at this reality is not to wallow in it; rather, it is to offer an understanding of why First Nations individuals, families, and communities continue to struggle socially, economically, and spiritually. For ourselves it is emancipating and empowering; for non-First Nations people it can be enlightening and empowering as you begin to understand the truth about our shared history and how it affects all of our lives.

1867 British North America Act

Ah, 1867 – the year the full-on formal imposition of European laws and policies all began with the implementation of the *British North American Act* (*BNA Act*), later re-named the *Canadian Constitution Act*. The year the provinces of Canada, Nova Scotia, and New Brunswick formed the Dominion of Canada. In doing so, the British Crown unilaterally declared their legislative authority over Indians and lands reserved for Indians in Section 91(24) of the *BNA Act*. The *BNA Act* and the *Indian Act* which followed in 1876 would become the basis for the political and legal relationship between Canada and First Nations people. This, despite the fact that First Nations people did not knowingly enter into any such arrangement to forfeit their inherent rights to their land and resources, much less their autonomy as the first people of what became Canada. The 1996 Royal Commission on Aboriginal People documented that some individual Nations purposefully aligned themselves with the British or the French, but none ever knowingly fully ceded their rights, land, or resources. The report notes further that both the French and English were well aware that there were many individual 'Indian' Nations that were autonomous. This is evident in how they interacted with each Nation through specific alliances and/or treaties. So, Canada was formed under the false pretences that it had the cooperation and assent of the many individual First Nations – Nations that had already been here for a very long time. And so began the wholesale implementation of laws and policies that would govern the day-to-day lives of First Nations people. To this day we struggle to assert our inherent rights to the land, resources, and ourselves.

Find Out More

2010 Annotated Indian Act and Aboriginal Constitutional Provisions. Shin Imai, Editor. Carswell. 2009.

The Report of the Royal Commission on Aboriginal People. 1996.

Indian Act

The *Indian Act* is the primary piece of federal legislation that governs Status Indians and most aspects of their day-to-day lives including governance, Band membership and elections, home ownership, land use and ownership, taxation, use of natural resources, and their relationship with the Government of Canada. The federal government's self-defined authority to create the *Indian Act* was found in Section 91(24) of the *1867 Constitution Act* which declared that Canada would be responsible for 'Indians and lands reserved for Indians'. The passing of the first *Indian Act* in 1876 consolidated and expanded upon previous legislation such as the 1869 *Act for the Gradual Enfranchisement of Indians*. Such legislation supported and justified the westward expansion of the country, the federal government's increased efforts to secure land by entering into treaties with individual Nations, and to assimilate First Nations people into European society and values. There have been many changes to the *Indian Act* throughout the years, with major overhauls taking place in 1951 and 1985, but the basic underlying principles of assimilation and control over many aspects of First Nations people's lives remain intact.

The introduction of the *Indian Act* ensured that "The Department was empowered to institute all the systems of development it cherished: individualized land holding, education and resource and financial management. Subsequent Acts ... blanketed communities with regulations in an attempt to establish Canadian economic and social norms throughout community life." (Indian Act Colonialism: A Century Of Dishonour: 1869-1969. John Milloy. 2008. p. 7). The *Indian Act* defined who was an 'Indian', replaced traditional governance models with elected or appointed male Band Councils, limited what economic activity we could participate in, and included ways that individuals could involuntarily lose their Indian status such as obtaining a university degree or becoming a lawyer. Milloy notes that despite the stated goal of assimilating First

Nations people into mainstream society, successive policies implemented by the federal government would place First Nations people at a great disadvantage as they were forced onto remote reserves and "left to find their own way forward with little federal assistance. For almost all communities this became an increasingly insurmountable challenge, particularly in the first half of the 20th century as the nation modernized, becoming industrialized in urban and in rural areas." (Milloy. ibid. p 5.)

Between 1876 and its first overhaul in 1951 there were many amendments to the *Indian Act* that increased the federal government's control over First Nations people's lives and the efforts to assimilate us into mainstream society. Notable additions include the banning of ceremonies such as the potlatch and ghost dance (1884), the power to remove Indians from reserves near towns with more than 8,000 people (1905), powers to expropriate land from Bands without consent (1911), requiring western Indians to obtain official permission to appear in public in traditional 'costumes' (1914), government leasing of unfarmed reserve lands to non-Indians without consultation or consent (1918), restricting fundraising for land claims (1927), and allowing Indian agents to run Band Council meetings and to cast a tie-breaking vote if needed (1936).

Major changes to the *Indian Act* in 1951 included the creation of a central registry that defined who was entitled to be recognized as a Status Indian, the lifting of the ban on activities associated with making a land claim or practicing cultural traditions, and women being forced to give up their Indian status when they married a non-status man (Indian or non-Indian). We were then allowed to sell or slaughter livestock without a permit, thus allowing us to make a few of our own economic decisions. The 1951 *Indian Act* also introduced the authority of provinces to implement laws where federal ones did not exist, which led to provinces instituting child welfare laws that would lead to large numbers of First Nations children being separated from their families and traditions. For more information see the section 'Child Welfare ... Or Warfare?'

The first major change to the *Indian Act* brought about by direct action from First Nations groups came in 1985 with the passage of *Bill C-31,* which granted control of Band membership to Bands and removed specific sections that did not comply with the equality provisions of the *Canadian Charter of Rights and Freedoms*. The offending sections dealt with the passing on or loss of Indian status through females. Despite the removal of those sections, the *Indian Act* continues to discriminate against women. This reality led lawyer Sharon McIvor to launch a *Charter of Rights and Freedoms* challenge of *Bill C-31* based on sex and marriage. Ms. McIvor's 20 year effort led to the B.C. Supreme Court directing the Government of Canada to amend the *Indian Act* by April 2010.

It was estimated that Ms. McIvor's perseverance would result in as many as 45,000 people regaining their Indian status. However, Ms. McIvor's victory soon turned sour when it became clear that the federal government intended on forcing through their own remedy via *Bill C-3* (*Gender Equity in Indian Registration Act*), even though it was opposed by many First Nations organizations and Bands and will likely result with few people regaining their Indian status. Ms. McIvor, the Native Women's Association of Canada (NWAC), and others note that *Bill C-3* is not the correct remedy as it will only affect those who were born after September 4, 1951. Ms. McIvor says that "the only way to be sure that sex discrimination is totally and finally eliminated from the status registration scheme is to place descendants of status Indian women, that is matrilineal descendants, on the same footing as descendants of status Indian men." (Sharon McIvor's Response to the August 2009 Proposal of Indian and Northern Affairs Canada to Amend the 1985 *Indian Act*). Ms. McIvor has since filed a complaint with the United Nations Human Rights Committee against Canada regarding this ongoing discrimination against First Nations women. Despite these important concerns, *Bill C-3* came into force on January 31, 2011.

Another amendment to the *Indian Act* was a result of the

1999 Corbiere case which successfully challenged section 77(1) of the *Indian Act* which required Band members to be "ordinarily resident" on reserve to vote in Band elections. This decision of the Supreme Court of Canada led to the 2000 amendment to the *Indian Act* that resulted in off-reserve Band members gaining the right to vote in Band elections and referendums.

> *"The Indian Act is not working. It was never designed for the success of our people or our communities. It had nothing to do with what we wish for our future or our children. If anybody's gonna [change it], we have to."*
>
> Herb George, NCFNG President

Since the 1980s, the Government of Canada has negotiated various levels of self-government with individual Bands which would partially or fully free them from the grip of the *Indian Act*. However, it wasn't until the mid-1990s that an official policy was implemented that allowed for Aboriginal self-government. Despite this new direction, most of the 614 First Nations Bands are still governed by the *Indian Act* which continues to be a lightning rod for relations between First Nations and the Government of Canada. Both would like to get rid of the *Indian Act*, but by different means and for different reasons. The Assembly of First Nations (AFN), the National Center for First Nations Governance (NCFNG), and NWAC still struggle to eliminate the *Indian Act* and its inherently patriarchal and sexist control of our daily lives in favor of self-government on a Nation to Nation basis with the Government of Canada. In July 2010, the AFN National Chief called for the elimination of the *Indian Act* within five years. The AFN believes this can happen by creating a joint First Nations and federal working group that would develop a plan to confirm First Nations' rights and title, retain existing funding levels through transfer agreements to Bands, and by assisting Bands to strengthen their administration in preparation for self-governance. However, our leaders tread with great caution to ensure that the Government of Canada does not whittle away our inherent and treaty rights as First Nations people in the process. We have experienced more than enough of a history of broken treaties, unfulfilled promises, and one-sided agreements with the federal government to know not to rush into anything without thoroughly reviewing it and assessing its long-term impacts.

Find Out More

Aboriginal Women and Bill C-31. Native Women's Association of Canada. 2007.
Bill C-31: Act to Amend the Indian Act. Government of Canada. 1985.
Exploratory Process on Indian Registration, Band Membership and Registration: An Overview. Native Women's Association of Canada. 2011.
Bill C-3: Gender Equity in Indian Registration Act. Government of Canada. 2010.
Governance Best Practices Report. National Centre for First Nations Governance. 2009.
Bill C-7: The First Nations Governance Act. Government of Canada.
Indian Act Colonialism: A Century Of Dishonour: 1869-1969. John Milloy. National Centre for First Nations Governance. 2008.
Seven Generations, Seven Teachings: Ending The Indian Act. John Borrows. National Center for First Nations Governance. 2008.
An Indian Act: Shooting the Indian Act. Lawrence Paul Yuxweluptun. Grunt Gallery.
Union of BC Indian Chiefs Historic Timeline: From 1700 to the Present.
The Indian Act. Mary C. Hurley. Government of Canada. Library of Parliament. 2009.
Aboriginal Self-Government. Mary C. Hurley. Government of Canada. Library of Parliament. 2009.

Spotlight – Shooting the Indian Act

Many people ask why we don't just get rid of the *Indian Act*. Well it just isn't that easy when First Nations and the Government of Canada are continents apart. We know that we have an inherent right to govern ourselves, but the government is trying to impose another patriarchal act. We know our traditional governance structures have great value, but the government says we need more colonial systems. We say, quit trampling on our rights, while the government is telling Canadians they are attempting to protect our human rights. Although many groups are working on this issue, the *Indian Act* will likely die a slow death. What if it were as simple as killing the *Indian Act*? Well, Lawrence Paul Yuxweluptun did try. In order to physically demonstrate his feelings about the *Indian Act*, he traveled to its colonial birthplace – Britain – to metaphorically kill the *Indian Act* by shooting it with a rifle. If only it were that easy.

Reserves

The creation of reserves goes back to before the formation of Canada. The *Royal Proclamation* of 1763 required the negotiation of treaties with Indian Nations before any claims or title to land could be extinguished. Despite the existence of this proclamation, vast amounts of land were taken prior to the signing of treaties to either create reserves for Indians or to give or sell land to non-Indian people. Various policies and treaties called for different amounts of land to be allotted to each First Nations person or family; however, that obligation was often not honored fully or in some cases at all. One example is Treaty 8 in northern Alberta which called for 128 acres of land per person up to a maximum of 640 acres per family of five or 160 acres for each person who wanted to sever their ties to the Band and live on their own land separate from the reserve. The majority of land that was supposed to be allocated to Bands often was not. In addition, large amounts of reserve land was later expropriated without any negotiation, consultation, explanation, compensation, or sometimes without Bands even being aware. First Nations across the country are still in the midst of formal land claims with the Government of Canada over lands that were taken illegally and/or without compensation.

There are over 600 reserves scattered across Canada. These small plots of land are nowhere near what First Nations were promised in the first treaties and agreements with Canada and most reserves are in remote areas, are on non-agricultural land, and do not have the infrastructure of roads, sewage, and hydro to adequately serve those who live on them. Various opinions abound about the intentions of those who allotted the reserve lands. Assertions include that the reserves were in remote locations because they wanted to protect settlers from the uncivilized Indians; they wanted to keep First Nations people segregated until their gradual civilization and assimilation after which they would be allowed to mix amongst the settlers; or First Nations people were just given what was thought to be the worst land. Later requirements for railway lines and highways, discoveries of underground and underwater natural resources, and other needs of the growing nation state of Canada and its settlers believed to be more important than the First Nations' needs would lead to more expropriation of land and displacement of First Nations people.

Reserve lands are reserved for Status Indians but they do not own the land; rather, these lands are held in trust by the Government of Canada. Ironically, the creation of reserves ultimately acted against the government's attempts at assimilation as First Nations people were able to maintain somewhat insulated communities and a land base from which to retain our culture and communities. In late 2010, the First Nations Tax Commission hosted the First Nations Property Ownership Conference in an effort to push forward a First Nations fee simple individual land ownership model to free up 'dead capital'. This idea has been floated over the years under the guise of a good economic alternative for First Nations people. Those who advocate for the change in land ownership simply view land as a commodity that can create capital whereas most First Nations people view individual ownership as a great threat to First Nations' inherent treaty and communal rights to our land base. Community activist, Arthur Manuel describes it best by stating that "no single individual can give up or extinguish our Aboriginal Title and Indigenous Rights. It would be suicide or extinguishment for our future generations to accept Fee Simple in exchange for our collective Title."

In the United States, there over 500 Tribes, but only about 300 reservations as some Tribes are landless or share land with other Tribes. Their lands are called reservations, not reserves as they are in Canada. The U.S. has enacted various laws over the years that have opened up reservation lands to various types of ownership including individual and Tribe ownership. Also there are both federal and state reservations in the U.S., while in Canada there are only federal reserves.

Canada/USA Border – Nationhood

One of the most important consequences of creating the Canada/USA border is that many First Nations families and communities were torn apart in the process. When this arbitrary line was drawn to meet the needs of the settlers, First Nations people were not consulted. Today, all along the border there are people who belong to the same family and Nation who are divided by the Canada/USA border. This imposed border severely restricts their movement back and forth between Canada and the United States. First Nations people were used to travelling without restriction to and from communities for family functions, to attend cultural ceremonies, or to trade, gather food, fish, or hunt. Today, First Nations people all along the border are forced to stop and prove their citizenship before they can visit their family or attend a cultural event on the other side.

The creation of the border also imposed significant social and economic consequences for those caught on either side. Depending on which side of the border you live on, an individual's, community's, or Nation's health, freedom, economic opportunities, and many other important things are far different and more restricted than for their family on the other side of the border. Other significant areas that have great differences include how treaties are made, interpreted and implemented, or what type of health care, education, or training is available to a First Nations person living in either country.

The creation of the border created two countries, and First Nations people were forced to become part of one. It is true that many Nations had signed treaties, but that was for a working relationship with newcomers, not to cede their right to be self-governing in their traditional territories. To this day, many First Nations people do not consider themselves either Canadian or American. For these individuals the primary reason for their refusal to be called one or the other is based on their belief that First Nations people have never fully given up their territory or their inherent right to govern themselves within what became

Canada or the United States. Therefore, many find it impossible to take on the name 'Canadian' or 'American', despite the fact that we live within the country's borders. Rather, many refer to ourselves by our Nation (Tsimshian, Cree, Saulteaux) and/or as an Indigenous person to North America. Some people tend to over-simplify this important belief by asking questions like "then why do you cheer for Team Canada?" This is based on a patriotic world view that if your country's team is competing, you better be cheering for them as if you're not with them you're against them. Many First Nations people may cheer for Team Canada during the Olympic Games, but if Team Canada were to compete against their First Nations team, First Nations people would overwhelmingly cheer for their First Nations team. A person's appreciation of a particular sports team does not necessarily mean an allegiance to the country that they represent.

The Haudenosaunee in the northeastern United States have taken their citizenship as Haudenosaunee very seriously. So much so that they developed their own passport which has been recognized for over 30 years as a legal passport for international travel. However, their rights were quickly trampled upon in the summer of 2010. To meet the needs of the 'War on Terror', the Iroquois Nationals Lacrosse Team was left stranded in New York waiting to travel to England for the World Lacrosse Championships. The U.S. government refused to guarantee that they would be allowed back into the U.S. upon return with their Haudenosaunee passports despite having accepted the passport since 1977. Eventually, the team was given a one-time waiver by the U.S., but the United Kingdom refused to recognize the Haudenosaunee passport as valid travel documents. The team stood strong to their beliefs by refusing to agree that they were not a independent Nation of self-governing people by giving into pressure to also produce a U.S. passport. The high ranking team was forced to withdraw from the championship. Confederacy secretary Jessica Shenandoah summed it up by stating that the "border has been imposed on us right in the middle of our territory. We are not U.S. nor Canadian citizens."

Residential Schools

> *"Two primary objectives of the Residential Schools system were to remove and isolate children from the influence of their homes, families, traditions and cultures, and to assimilate them into the dominant culture ... Indeed, some sought, as it was infamously said, "to kill the Indian in the child."*
>
> Prime Minister of Canada. 2008.

Indian residential schools were set up across the country as Canada's largest effort to assimilate First Nations people into mainstream society. Over 150,000 children were forcibly removed from their family and community and sent to one of 130 residential schools in order to stop the transmission of cultural beliefs and practices. In their place, First Nations children were to learn how to fit into mainstream society by converting them to Christianity, and teaching them how to behave in an acceptable way, to speak English, and some basic working skills. Residential schools operated across Canada for over 100 years, with the last one closing its doors in Saskatchewan in 1996. For the most part, the Government of Canada contracted out the operations of residential schools to the Roman Catholic, Anglican, Methodist, United, and Presbyterian churches. It has been publicly acknowledged by the churches that ran the residential schools, as well as the Government of Canada, that most children who lived in these schools faced ongoing physical, mental, sexual, emotional, and spiritual abuses during their attendance. Rather than teaching them their ABCs and 123s, they were taught negative behaviours and coping mechanisms. They were taught that punishment was okay and expected, how to ridicule, a skewed sense of sexuality, homophobia, and that it was not good to be a First Nations person or to speak our traditional languages. Some of our greatest losses included parenting skills, healthy coping mechanisms, cultural practices, our languages, trust, a normal childhood, a sense of safety and belonging, healthy and supportive First Nations communities, a healthy sense of sexuality, and a natural connection to the Creator that was not based on fear and damnation.

In addition to residential schools, many other First Nations children were sent to Indian Day Schools in their home community where they faced the same abuses and challenges as residential school survivors did. The main difference was that day school survivors were able to go home at night, only to return to school the following morning. The illustration on the next page clearly shows how the current and future generations of First Nations people will continue to bear the effects of the Government of Canada's attempt to civilize and assimilate us into mainstream society. In both cases, when priests or others were accused of sexually abusing children, or known to sexually abuse children, they were simply moved to another school where they continued to sexually abuse children rather than being defrocked and criminally charged.

It has been widely acknowledged that the effects of these horrific places still significantly impact First Nations individuals, families, and communities as most children were in the schools for at least 10 years, and as many as seven successive generations were forced to live in these schools. It did not just happen in one community or province; rather, it was forced upon an entire people with over 150,000 children legally forced to attend. Now imagine that this happened to your family, going back over 100 years. What do you think your life would be like now if all of your ancestors were subjected to such abuses and stripped of your support systems and coping mechanisms generation after generation? If you can imagine this, you can understand what our reality is and maybe have a general idea of what needs to be accomplished in order to change it for the better. First Nations communities continue to struggle, mostly on their own, to recover from this dark Canadian legacy.

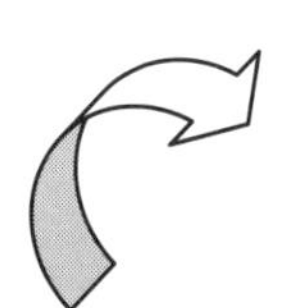

Remove children from their family, culture and support systems

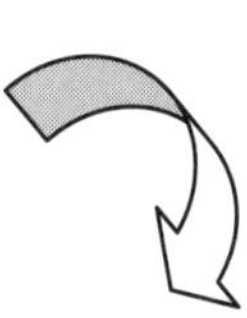

Send the children home to parents who were taught the same unhealthy behaviors

Disrupt cultural, spiritual, coping, and healing practices

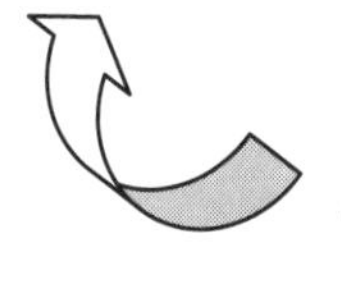

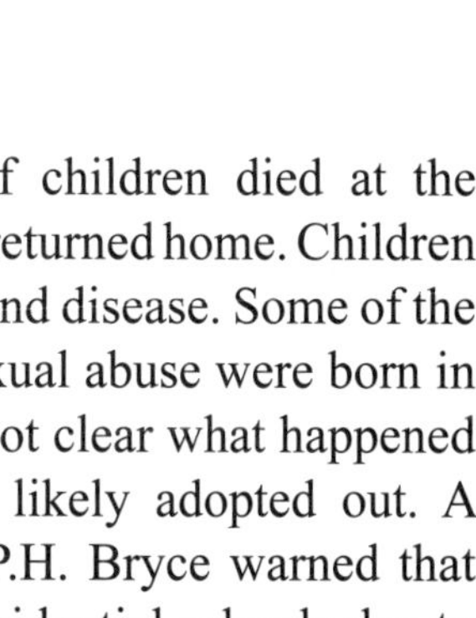

Shame, punish, and abuse helpless children

Estimates are that thousands of children died at the residential schools and many were never returned home. Children died from malnutrition, physical abuse, and disease. Some of the babies who were conceived from the sexual abuse were born in residential schools and died there. It is not clear what happened to those babies who lived; they were likely adopted out. A 1907 report by Chief Medical Officer P.H. Bryce warned that 15-24% of all children were dying in residential schools due to malnutrition, disease, and poor living conditions (numbers rose to 42% for children who were sent home to die). His warnings to make improvements were ignored and many more children died needlessly for decades.

Many people insist that even though there were abuses in the residential schools, the Government of Canada's and the churches' efforts were for good reason and our children were at least educated to fit into the new society. The true goal in creating residential schools can best be illustrated by reviewing whether or not they actually educated First Nations people. It has been documented that many of the schools only taught children to as low as Grade 3. Most of these children's time was spent cleaning, doing laundry, reading the bible, and doing menial tasks that the operators of the schools did not want to do themselves. Those who were taught some work skills that could be useful to them once they were released, were quite fortunate. However, most were taught skills that were not useful to them in terms of earning enough money to feed themselves and their families. Some children from remote areas or non-agricultural lands were taught how to farm even though they would not be able to use those skills upon returning home. Sadly, many survivors could not read or write enough English to get a job, much less teach their children or grandchildren how to read or write.

Find Out More

A National Crime: The Canadian Government and the Residential School System. John S. Milloy. 1999.
Broken Circle: The Dark Legacy of Indian Residential Schools: A Memoir. Theodore Fontaine. Heritage House. 2010.
Is Sorry Enough (song). Murray Porter.
Massacre: A Survey of Today's American Indian (Flogging Children chapter). Robert Gessner. 1932.
National Residential School Survivors' Society Newsletter
The Circle Game: Shadows and Substance in the Indian Residential School Experience in Canada. R. Chrisjohn and S. Young. Revised Edition. Theytus Books. 2006.
Unsettling the Settler Within: Indian Residential Schools, Truth Telling, and Reconciliation in Canada. Paulette Regan. UBC Press. 2010.

Child Welfare … Or Warfare?

Once it became clear that the colonizing nations would not be able to defeat or suppress First Nations people and our traditional cultural ways, a new tactic was introduced – take away the children. This new war game was an assimilationist tool which the Canadian and American governments thought would make it easier to forcibly convert us to Christianity and Euro-centric ways of being, while stripping away our 'Indianness'. It was believed that disrupting the transmission of cultural beliefs and practices to future generations was the best way to break us down and make it easier to assimilate us into mainstream society. Of course, the beginning of this was done in the name of education through residential schools (see the section 'Residential Schools'). The later tool of assimilation was for governments to seize our children under the guise of 'protecting them.' The intent was clear, and the ongoing effects continue to be devastating.

The 60s Scoop

Although residential schools began to shut their doors in the 1950s, they would continue to negatively affect First Nations people in many ways. All of the negative behaviors that we learned in residential schools helped to reinforce non-First Nations people's claims that we were incapable of caring for our own children. Rather than acknowledge the devastation that it had imposed on our communities and provide opportunities for us to start the long road of recovery, the Government of Canada ignored the devastation it had created and left us to wallow in our pain and suffering in extreme poverty and isolation.

At the same time as the residential schools began to close, the 1951 changes to the *Indian Act* gave the provinces the authority to create laws and policy where federal ones did not exist. Individual provinces began to implement laws that made it possible to continue separating us from our children. In British Columbia this was done soon after the first residential school closed in B.C. The child welfare laws that were created were based on Euro-centric beliefs which were opposite to First Nations' traditional ways of being. Even when there were actual safety issues within the home, there were no supports given to our families to recover from generations of abuse and neglect in the residential schools or to adjust to these new and foreign expectations which were generally just different, not better, for children.

During the 1960s, thousands of First Nations children were taken into 'care' by the provinces and put into foster homes supposedly for their protection – this is known as 'The 60's Scoop'. New generations of First Nations children were taken from their families and being abused at the hands of others, with no hope of returning home. Despite lobbying by First Nations people to have access to resources equal to government agencies to care for our own children, there has been no meaningful change in the last five decades to help us keep our families together. Today, there continues to be a large over-representation of First Nations children in the custody of the provinces. In fact, there are more of our children in foster care today than there were children taken away at the height of the residential schools. The First Nations Child and Family Caring Society of Canada (FNCFCSC) reports that many First Nations children are apprehended due to issues such as poverty and neglect rather than maltreatment, which is in contrast to non-First Nations people's experience. FNCFCSC believes that these risk factors can be meaningfully addressed if the proper resources – such as alcohol and drug treatment and skills development – were more readily available to First Nations people where they live. FNCFCSC also notes that on-reserve First Nations agencies receive only 72% of the funding levels that non-First Nations agencies do. In 2010, the Canadian Council of Provincial Child and Youth Advocates released *Aboriginal Children and Youth in Canada: Canada Must Do Better* which highlighted the social disparities for First Nations children across the country caused by inter-generational disadvantage and a lack of a coordinated federal effort to help alleviate those conditions. The federal and provincial governments have been aware for many years of the disparities in outcomes and funding to help support First Nations children. However, we still await a coordinated and fully funded effort to create meaningful change for the most vulnerable population in the country.

Adoption out of First Nations Communities

In addition to taking our children away from their families and communities and placing them into foster homes, child welfare agencies started to adopt our children into non-First Nations homes, and outside of the country, at a very fast pace. This loss of children added to the devastation that had already been tearing apart our communities as there was no more hope that these children would ever return home as children, if at all. Often the children who were adopted out never knew that they were First Nations people, but were often treated badly by others because they were First Nations. Many of these children never found their way home to their families and communities.

Find Out More

Stolen From Our Embrace: The Abduction of First Nations Children and the Restoration of Aboriginal Communities. Suzanne Fournier and Ernie Crey. Douglas & McIntyre. 1998.

Liberating Our Children, Liberating Our Nations. The Committee. 1992.

The Circle Game: Shadows and Substance in the Indian Residential School Experience in Canada. R. Chrisjohn and S. Young. Theytus Books. 2006.

Aski Awasis/Children of the Earth: First Peoples Speaking on Adoption. Editor, Jeanine Carriere. Fernwood Publishing. 2010.

Aboriginal Children and Youth in Canada: Canada Must Do Better. Canadian Council of Provincial Child and Youth Advocates. 2010.

Politics – Indian Act & Mainstream

Politics for First Nations people comes in many forms, and each person's level of involvement and/or belief in it varies. Every person's day-to-day life is affected by mainstream politics, but First Nations people, whether status or not, experience additional impacts from processes and policies that flow out of the *Indian Act* and the *Canadian Constitution*. First Nations people's lives are influenced by both on-reserve *Indian Act* politics and mainstream politics at all levels, including the policies and actions that are related to our inherent rights as First Nations people which are enshrined in the *Constitution*.

Indian Act Politics

On-reserve politics are governed by the *Indian Act* which imposes an election-based system that has replaced our traditional forms of governance. While each Nation's governance systems may have differed, they were primarily based upon the best interest of the overall community. A leader's role was to best represent everyone's needs, not just their own as is more prevalent in today's political reality. Unfortunately, along with all of the troubles that have arisen from colonization and the residential school experiences, there are sometimes people who lack the moral and ethical strengths to be true leaders. One of the signs of an unhealthy community is when factions arise that are based upon family or other ties rather than political ideology or the best interest of a community. Some of these issues are being influenced by off-reserve voting which began after the Supreme Court of Canada ruled on the *Corbiere v. Canada* case.

The landmark *Corbiere* case affirmed that a Status Indian's rights are portable. Since they are portable, or can move with us, we have the right to nominate and vote for Band Council where we are registered members. It is also now possible for First Nations people living away from the reserve of which they are a member to run for Band Council. Of course this has both benefits and challenges. A few of the benefits include ensuring off-reserve members have an influence on how their home community is governed, that off-reserve members are able to access the resources that should be afforded to them, that there may be fewer elections that are won by the families or factions with the largest numbers, and that many off-reserve members have skills that might be in short supply on-reserve. Challenges include members not knowing who they are voting for, families or factions gaining more members to further skew voting, resources being unfairly directed towards off-reserve members and their initiatives, and the additional cost of Council members travelling to and from Band meetings on-reserve. Hopefully, communities will view this as an opportunity to embrace the inclusion of off-reserve members and their skills to help strengthen their community, rather than as a burden.

Self-Government

Many new treaties and land claims settlements include provisions for self-governance, which in most cases includes no longer being bound by the *Indian Act*. The first agreement was signed in 1975 with the Cree, Naskapi, and Inuit in northern Quebec under the James Bay and Northern Quebec Agreement, with only two other agreements being signed up to 1995. Since 1995, there have been several agreements signed with varying levels of self-governing powers (see the section 'Treaties'). Self-government, and the ensuing jurisdictional rights and powers remain a controversial subject in relation to non-First Nations people who believe that they should be consulted before and after the final agreements are signed. The National Centre for First Nations Governance is the leading authority on issues related to First Nations governance issues, research, and training. Their goal is to help Nations rebuild and re-establish their self governing, political, and economic systems to help return First Nations to their independent, prosperous, and healthy selves.

Mainstream Politics

On-reserve First Nations people (i.e. Status Indians) were not even considered to be Canadian citizens until 1956 when the *Canadian Citizenship Act* was passed. The new *Act* included retroactive citizenship back to 1947, which not so coincidently was prior to Canada's adoption of the Universal Declaration on Human Rights. Up until 1960, only Inuit, Métis, and non-status First Nations people were able to vote in federal elections. Prior to 1960, Status Indians could gain the right to vote by giving up their Indian status, but to do so would mean that they would have to leave their home community and they would not have medical coverage or many other important benefits.

Despite now having the right to vote in mainstream government elections, many of us choose not to. Of course, voting rates are sometimes higher in particular areas due to population size, if there is a First Nations candidate, or if there is a hot button issue that First Nations feel they can have influence on if they have a friendly member of government. However, for the most part, many First Nations people do not believe that we have any influence over mainstream politics. Many First Nations people do not vote for various reasons including a refusal to participate in a system that is forced upon us as the first people of what is now known as Canada, not feeling like our vote counts, not believing that the government cares about First Nations' issues or concerns, or not having been raised to understand the benefits of participating in the political system. I am of the opinion that if you don't vote, you don't matter to those who are running for office. Wealthy people are the best at the game of politics; they know that they must play the game in order to have a chance to win, and the more you know the game and use it to your advantage, the more you are paid attention to, and therefore benefit. I do not vote to fulfill my civic duty or to say I believe in the political system; rather, I vote to ensure that I have a voice.

Find Out More

The Timeline: A History of Our Inherent Right of Self-Governance. National Centre for First Nations Governance.
Aboriginal Governance: An Annotated Bibliography. National Centre for First Nations Governance.
Governance Best Practice Report. National Centre for First Nations Governance. 2009.
The Jurisdiction of Inherent Right Aboriginal Governments. National Centre for First Nations Governance. 2007.
The Government of Canada's Approach to Implementation of the Inherent Right and the Negotiation of Aboriginal Self-Government. Government of Canada.
Aboriginal Self-Government. Mary C. Hurley. Government of Canada. Library of Parliament. 2009.
To Vote or Not Vote: A Question of Sovereignty for Indigenous Peoples. Pam Palmater. Indigenous Nationhood Blog Site.

Cultural Appropriation

First Nations cultural objects, and even human remains, have been separated from First Nations people since the time of first contact with visitors to North America. This occurred through many means including theft, trade or sale. The 1876 *Indian Act,* which made the sundance, potlatch, ghost dance, and other First Nations ceremonies illegal, resulted in thousands of ceremonial objects, masks, and regalia being confiscated by government agents. Many of the objects were burned in public to scare those who did not want to comply with the ban, while others were sent to museums to preserve a small part of what the government hoped was a dying culture. In many cases, items were taken by Indian agents, priests, and others to keep or to sell for their own profit. Thousands of items are still in private collections around the world, while only a small portion has been repatriated to their communities through the hard work and dedication of community members.

First Nations images have also been appropriated and exploited since people first realized that they could make money from them. Our image was put on the American nickel in the 1930s as a way to commemorate the passing of a way of life. First Nations images are misused for profit on coins, stamps, medicine bottles, candy, food items, cars, alcohol, and many other commercial items. You can now buy First Nations art pieces that have been mass manufactured across the ocean for sale around the world. You can buy a dream catcher key ring, Kokopelli t-shirt, or beaded bracelet at your local flea market or dollar store, but it will not be an authentic First Nations piece of art that has been made with cultural integrity, materials, and pride. During the 2010 Winter Olympics in Vancouver, some artists started buyaboriginal.com to make a statement about the authenticity of First Nations art being distributed at the Games and the exclusion of many First Nations artists despite the promise of meaningful inclusion of First Nations art and artists throughout the Games. They encourage people to ask questions when buying First Nations art or other products to identify whether they are authentically made and distributed by First Nations people.

In other cases, cultural ceremonies and practices are used for profit without the consent of those who are authorized to give it. Wild Bill Hickok, movie producers, and wrestling shows have all profited from using First Nations people, or people pretending to be us, to draw crowds. Drum circles, sweatlodges, and pow-wows are all being appropriated to make a quick buck from those who don't know or care that it is not an authentic ceremony run by First Nations people. The most blatant case of this, which also led to great tragedy, involves the author of *The Secret,* James Arthur Ray, who reportedly charges up to $10,000 per week for a retreat which includes a sweatlodge ceremony in a greatly over-sized replica of a real sweatlodge. Internationally, cultural camps and pow-wows are offered in countries such as Germany. The Boys Scouts of America website invites members to "get ready to move your feet, catch your rhythm, and awake your principal at Indian Summer" as they pretend to be First Nations people. High school, college, and professional sports teams use First Nations images for their crests and mascots despite many years of opposition from First Nations groups such as the National Congress of American Indians. First Nations opposition is strongest in areas where their images, mascots, and accompanying activities are cartoon-like and a parody of authentic First Nations actions and ceremonies.

Human remains are not just a pile of bones to First Nations people; they are sacred. While we have an understanding that our body is just a vessel for our spiritual selves, we also understand that our body is a gift from the Creator that must be cared for even after death. There are many ceremonies that surround the care of a body after death that must be adhered to. We are people who are inherently tied to the land and the places that our ancestors walked, so for many of us it is extremely important that our final resting place be in our traditional territories, not in museum drawers where many remains are kept for scientific study. In 1990, the American Government passed the *Native American Graves Protection and Repatriation Act* (*NAGPRA*) to help return human remains, funerary objects, sacred objects, and objects of cultural patrimony to their original family or Tribe. The *Act* includes penalties for non-compliance and illegal trafficking of these items, as well as some grants to help Tribes identify and repatriate objects and human remains. Although not everyone is required to report the numbers of repatriations through or because of *NAGPRA*, as of 2009, the U.S. Department of the Interior had records of repatriation for 38,671 human remains, over one million funerary objects, 4,303 sacred objects, 948 objects of cultural patrimony, and 822 objects that are both sacred and patrimonial. First Nations people estimate that this is just a small fraction of the items that were taken and yet to be returned. Many Tribes are utilizing *NAGPRA* to force museums to return human remains and cultural items; however, the process is slow and cumbersome so it can take years, and in some cases may not happen at all if government-defined proof is not provided. It is very frustrating for the Tribes to know that their ancestors remain locked away in museum basements (often in drawers or boxes) while they wade through red tape. Canada has no legislation regarding the repatriation of cultural items, or even human remains. Most major Canadian museums have policies regarding repatriation, but they are not enforceable by First Nations people. Despite the fact that First Nations people would, and still do, have different beliefs and practices regarding our cultural objects and human remains, we are often denied repatriation as our ability to properly care for the items is judged on a mainstream system that says that objects must be kept preserved forever in specific lighting and air circulation. People like to insist that colonization is over, but we are still forced to adhere to these policies despite their vast difference from our own beliefs surrounding the items that were most often stolen from us. On the Northwest Coast, totem poles were left to decompose naturally and return to the land, rather than being preserved forever.

EVERYTHING IS FOR SALE

Find Out More

Native American Graves Protection and Repatriation Act. U.S. Department of the Interior. 1990.

Turning the Page: Forging New Partnerships Between Museums and First Peoples. Assembly of First Nations and Canadian Museums Association. 1992.

www.buyaboriginal.com

National Congress of American Indians: Anti-Defamation and Mascots.

Anthropology

Anthropology was developed by and is predominantly practiced by white, male researchers. They seem to be the ones most interested in finding out where people come from, how their culture evolved, what their physical characteristics are, and many other Euro-centric curiosities. For many people, this is not important. There are a few major problems with anthropology in relation to First Nations people. First, anthropologists most often watch from afar and impose their own definition of what is happening or has happened from their own worldview. Second, if anthropologists are not from within a culture, or have some sense of what that culture entails or represents, they usually cannot appreciate or interpret what it is, much less understand its benefits to a community. Third, anthropology is based on one worldview for the most part, a Euro-centric one. This tunnel vision does not allow for a true understanding of what different cultures have to offer, and anthropologists tend to learn *about* other cultures, rather than *from* them. When working with diverse cultures, anthropologists would do well by acting as facilitators rather than imposing their archaic processes on us.

Dr. Beatrice Medicine and Dr. Vine Deloria Jr. both struggled for decades to highlight these important issues. They were effective to some extent, but much more work must be done to change the way anthropology impacts First Nations people. Their hard work has inspired many people, including my daughter Robin, to fight to Indigenize anthropology, or at least to stop it from bringing further harm to our communities. Dr. Linda Tuhiwai Smith noted the importance of Indigenizing research in her book *Decolonizing Methodologies*. She lays a good foundation to meaningfully analyze the benefits of anthropology for First Nations people or by First Nations people. If anthropology is going to survive in the 21st century as a meaningful discipline, it must evolve into something that works better for those who are being studied.

There are very few First Nations people who enter

into the field of anthropology. While it is not imperative that there be more students in anthropology and practicing it, it is imperative to have the First Nations' worldview incorporated into anthropology as a whole. It would be great to have more First Nations people in anthropology so that they can learn from others and teach others about anthropology from a First Nations' point of view, but it would be even greater if anthropology were redeveloped to better reflect the multi-ethnic reality of the world. As anthropology acknowledges, it is important to learn *about* other cultures, but they do not necessarily value the fact that they can also learn *from* other cultures. This Euro-centric view continues to stifle the field of anthropology and its students. Incorporating new ideas, methods, and voices is essential to making anthropology more relevant and useful to all people in these modern times, not just the academic field of anthropology. Imagine the world we could create if anthropology and other disciplines were open to learning from other cultures to help improve our fast growing inter-twined global societies.

Anthropology at its best helps people to better understand and embrace diverse cultures and how those cultures can help make the world a better place. At its worst, it is Euro-centrically biased and/or used against First Nations people by those who work to prove that we were not the first inhabitants of what is now known as North America. As each new theory is given credence, everyone jumps to use it to their own particular advantage. The problem with this is that they are only theories. We do not know that carbon dating or genetic mapping are reliable. We have seen the land bridge theory ebb and flow from the great answer to migration to a mere possibility of being part of the answer of how the world evolved. In recent years, there has been speculation that First Nations people came by canoe from Asia. Most First Nations people do not believe these theories, as we believe in our own creation stories that have been passed down by our ancestors through the generations. In the meantime, many generations of non-First Nations people have held steadfast to the land bridge theory as the absolute truth.

This is the problem with science which sometimes goes beyond our collective knowledge and skill; it is quite often seriously questioned as being correct or is disproved many years later after it has already influenced another generation or two. In the meantime, those who wish to prove something about someone else, use science like a weapon. This can be seen regularly in the U.S. where people often try to disprove First Nations' rights and title to the land through science. This is overwhelmingly driven by greed for resources, not science. So I ask all anthropologists and scientists to think twice before distributing information that can damage others, even if your only intent is good from your perspective and need.

Find Out More

Learning to be an Anthropologist and Remaining "Native". Dr. Beatrice Medicine. University of Illinois Press. 2001.
Evolution, Creationism, and Other Modern Myths: A Critical Inquiry, Dr. Vine Deloria Jr. Fulcrum Publishing 2002.
Decolonizing Methodologies: Research and Indigenous People. Dr. Linda Tuhiwai Smith. Zed Books. 1999.
Decolonizing Anthropology: Moving Further Toward an Anthropology for Liberation. Faye V. Harrison. Association of Black Anthropologists American Anthropological Association. 2nd edition. 1997.

Land Bridge – Myth or Reality?

While many scientists are focused on archeological evidence that they believe can explain how and when First Nations people first inhabited North America, we know that many of our creation stories are tied to North America. Other than the Inuit who report that their ancestors moved from Eastern Siberia to Alaska 5,000 year ago, many Nations call this land Turtle Island as their creation stories include a turtle turning into the land mass that is now known as North America. Noted scholar Vine Deloria Jr. stated that the "Sioux, Salish, and Cheyenne remember their life in the Far North" not from a migration from Asia and that "some tribal traditions do speak of ice and snow" and "begin with the supposition that these groups were already present in North America prior to the onset of glaciation".

Starting in the 1930s, scientists began speculating that First Nations people came to North America via a land bridge that connected North America to Siberia that was exposed during the last ice age as sea levels dropped dramatically. Theories continue that we originated in Asia and migrated to North America out of necessity as our ancestors followed their only food source, the woolly mammoth and bison as they traveled eastward. The thinking was that we later moved south as a corridor opened up when the ice began to melt and recede. This theory was seriously cast into doubt in the 1980s as scientists discovered more archeological evidence that made it impossible for us to have come during the time that the ice-free corridor was opened. This revelation spurred researchers to come up with alternate theories that either replaced or added to the land bridge theory. The most discussed hypothesis today is that our ancestors canoed over from Asia along the shoreline to the southern half of North America. The discovery of the 9,200 year old Kennewick Man, who scientist say resemble those of humans in Asia, and archeological evidence of at least 12,500 years old found on southern coastlines have led to attention being focused on this additional migration route. The belief that First Nations people are connected to Asia was fuelled by the examination of arrowheads and other artifacts that scientists note are similar to those found in Asia. Scientists acknowledge that this potential migration route is mostly speculation at this time as much of the archeological evidence was buried under water when the ice melted and ocean levels rose and eliminated shorelines. The lack of access to these artifacts inhibits scientists' ability to prove or disprove either the migration route or timelines. Currently, lots of attention is being paid to DNA evidence that reportedly ties some of us to Asia. Rico Newman and Georgetta Stonefish Ryan offer a logical alternative theory in *Do All Indians Live in Tipis?*, in that the land bridge "probably supported migration in both directions" thus leading to the similarities of artifacts and DNA as they were left in both places. This possibility is supported by theories that have animals such as horses and camels travelling over the land bridge to find a new home in Asia. So it is logical to conclude that humans would also have followed animals out of North American into Asia.

Vine Deloria Jr.'s review of modern literature on the land bridge theories calls into question their validity for a number of reasons, including his assertion that they have never been proven or seriously questioned, that it would be nearly impossible that humans or animals would have been willing or able to struggle over the many different mountain ranges to get to the land bridge and then survive the frozen tundra, and that First Nations people "as a general rule, have aggressively opposed the Bering Strait migration doctrine because it does not reflect any of the memories or traditions passed down by the ancestors over many generations". Many other prominent First Nations people, including Joy Harjo, Ward Churchill, Rico Newman, and Georgetta Stonefish Ryan speculate that the obsession with the land bridge theory is an attempt to prove that First Nations people were simply the first immigrants to North America which would absolve non-First Nations people of their guilt for stealing our lands. Most people will never believe history as First Nations people know it as their modern minds dismiss the notion that our creation stories are even possible. However, are the migration theories even possible given the evolving land bridge theory and limitations of science to prove it? When considering the lack of evidence or clear answers, there is one important question that we all should be asking which is why would First Nations people, whose very existence is based on oral history and honoring our ancestors, deny coming from somewhere else, and therefore, denying our heritage and betraying our ancestors?

To really exemplify my point, consider this – if the land bridge theory were true, the story of North American First Nations' inhabitation would go something like this:

> *After we made the arduous journey over several large mountain ranges and hiked thousands of miles over the land bridge, we all got together and discussed what might happen if others showed up someday, settled down, and then tried to deny us our rights as the First People of North America. So in order to protect ourselves, we all agreed to go our separate ways and develop our own cultures, similar but unique enough to prove we aren't all the same. Then each of the over 100 individual Nations decided to make up creations stories that revolve around North America so that we could prove that we weren't the first immigrants so we could protect our interests as the First People of this land.*

Wow, talk about a conspiracy theory!

<u>Find Out More</u>

Where Did Indians Come From?: How Did They Get To The Americas? Do All Indians Live in Tipis?: Questions & Answers from the National Museum of the American Indian. R. Newman and G. Stonefish Ryan. Harper Collins Publishing. 2007.

Low Bridge – Everybody Cross in Spirit & Reason: The Vine Deloria Jr. Reader. Vine Deloria Jr. Fulcrum Publishing. 1999.

"There is No Such Thing as a One-Way Land Bridge." Joy Harjo in Native Voices: American Indian Identity & Resistance. 2003.

Genocide or Not?

Many a debate has been waged about whether or not the newcomers and subsequent governments were trying to kill off all First Nations people. The claims of genocide are common, and defence against the accusation is swift and fierce. Maybe the problem is that people think *genocide* is the effort to completely kill off an entire people. The United Nations *Convention on the Prevention and Punishment of the Crime of Genocide (CPPCG)* Article II defines genocide as any "acts committed with intent to destroy, in whole or in part, a national, ethnical, racial or religious group." So even if there is no clear agreement that the Canadian or U.S. governments tried to exterminate First Nations people, there is overwhelming evidence of many acts of genocide that were levelled against us since the first wave of immigrants landed on our shores right up until recent times. The most relevant sections of the *CPPCG* that affirm this are "killing members of the group, imposing measures intended to prevent births within the group, and forcibly transferring children of the group to another group." So, it is clear to see that many of the atrocities that have been levelled against First Nations people were acts of genocide. A very compelling case can be made to show that there were many acts of genocide, even if there was no master plan to kill off all First Nations people.

One of the most common acts of genocide was the germ warfare which was carried out by distributing blankets and other supplies to First Nations people that were known to carry small pox. You can find evidence of this in the writings of those who care enough to highlight this important issue. They note that many first explorers and settlers reported in their journals or correspondence that this was a strategy that was used willingly.

Another despicable example was in 1907 when the Government of Canada Medical Examiner Peter Bryce wrote a report which clearly showed that up to 50% of First Nations children were dying in residential schools due to unsanitary conditions, a lack of attention and action regarding tuberculosis, and other reasons. Despite this damning evidence, the Government of Canada purposefully chose to ignore it and continued to operate residential schools as they had been for another few decades. Today, there are witnesses who are coming forward to tell about all of the children and babies who were buried on residential school grounds, but were never reported.

It is well known that doctors, on their own or by government mandate, purposefully and often secretly sterilized First Nations women in order to stop them from bearing children. The practice of eugenics, including some data on the over-representation of First Nations women, has been documented by many over the years.

The Beothuk of Newfoundland were literally hunted to extinction by newcomers who wanted their land and resources. Even though the Beothuk were known to be very passive and friendly, they were hunted down like animals until every last one was gone.

Those are some of the most blatant acts that can easily be defined as genocide. While there hasn't been any 'proof' that there was an overall plan to exterminate all First Nations people, there definitely were long-term initiatives to kill various First Nations populations that were at least hidden, ignored, and/or approved by governments. Reconciliation in this country cannot happen without full disclosure of all these atrocities, so that our common truths are known – then we can move forward with trust, respect, and a clear conscience.

Sidebar – Sterilization

The National Aboriginal Health Organization, the Native Women's Association of Canada, Andrea Smith, and others have documented the purposeful systematic sterilization of First Nations women in Canada and the U.S. throughout most of the 1900s. While no one has been able to identify the true extent of this atrocity, it is clear from estimates that First Nations women were much more likely to be sterilized without their consent or knowledge than other women. A 1974 study of the U.S. Indian Health Services by the Women of All Red Nations (WARN) revealed that "as many as 42 percent of all Indian women of childbearing age had by that point been sterilized without their consent." A General Accounting Office audit of Indian Health Services noted that in just four hospitals 3,406 First Nations women were involuntary sterilized from 1973-76, and records of the Government of Alberta's forced sterilizations showed that First Nations women were over-represented.

Most who speak about this note that First Nations women were sterilized to stop our population from increasing and because it was thought that we could not properly raise children. Some First Nations women were reportedly forced into having their 'tubes tied' by government officials who threatened to withhold funds they were entitled to receive. Many did not even know that they were sterilized; doctors simply did it without their knowledge. Who knows how many First Nations people there would have been if forced and secretive sterilizations has not happened. Recent literature by Jeannie Morgan, Andrea Smith, Marie Ralstin-Lewis, and others show that this problem still exists, only in a different form. Jeannie Morgan's analysis "reveals the ways in which international and Canadian texts construct the identity of young Indigenous women as a risk population in need of reproductive regulation." Andrea Smith has also found linkages between the over-prescribing of Depo-Provera to First Nations women in the United States even before it received FDA approval. Although there needs to be more research in this area, it is clear to some that the colonial process of regulating our reproduction is still active.

Find Out More

First Nations, Métis, and Inuit Women's Health. Yvonne Boyer. National Aboriginal Health Organization. 2006.

Depo-Provera and the Regulation of Indigenous Women's Reproduction. Jeannie Morgan. 2005.

Better Dead Than Pregnant: The Colonization of Native Women's Reproductive Health in Policing the National Body: Race, Gender and Criminalization. Andrea Smith. J. Silliman & A Bhatacharjee, Editors. 2002.

Killing The Seventh Generation. Esther Lucero and Dr. Melinda Micco. 2010.

The Continuing Struggle Against Genocide: Indigenous Women's Reproductive Rights. D. Maries and M. Ralstin-Lewis. Wicazo Sa Review: Journal of Native American Studies 20: 71-96. 2005.

Royal Commission on Aboriginal People

In 1991, seven commissioners were appointed to explore the issues relating to First Nations people and to then make recommendations to the Government of Canada. The report of the Royal Commission on Aboriginal People (RCAP) was released in 1996 after five years of consultations in 96 communities. The 4,000 page report is a proposed 20 year action plan that contained 440 recommendations that many First Nations leaders believed, if implemented, would greatly improve the living conditions of First Nations people and our relationship with the Government of Canada. Major aspects of the report included the recognition of First Nations peoples as self-governing Nations, the creation of new legislation and institutions, additional resources to First Nations people, fuller recognition of Métis people and their rights, First Nations authority over child welfare, increased spending to reach $1.5 billion per year by year five and then $2 billion per year over the next 15 years, and many other great things that are too many to account for here. Many First Nations people, international spectators, and Canadians were very happy with the report and eagerly awaited the Government of Canada's formal response with cautious optimism that things could change to help improve the strained relationship between First Nations people and the Government of Canada.

Much to the disappointment of First Nations people, international observers, and human rights activists it took over a year for the federal government to issue a formal response to the report. *Gathering Strength: Canada's Aboriginal Action Plan* was a great disappointment to all those who championed RCAP as a good vehicle to make meaningful progress on strengthening First Nations communities and their relationship with the federal government and Canadian society. The government's report including four broad objectives: renewing the partnership, strengthening First Nations governance, developing a new fiscal relationship, and Supporting Strong Communities, People and Economics. Overall, it was a watered down version of the RCAP report. This disappointment was bad enough, but the ensuing lack of meaningful action by the Government of Canada led to international reaction from the United Nations urging Canada to live up to their already limited commitments in *Gathering Strength*. There continued to be little progress made by the Government of Canada in ensuing years, and even less in recent years.

In 2006, the Assembly of First Nations released *Royal Commission on Aboriginal People at 10 Years: a Report Card*, which documented the Government of Canada's progress on RCAP. Overall, the Government of Canada received poor to failing marks in almost every category being analyzed. They received 1-A, 2-B+, 1-B-, 1-C+, 5-C, 6-C-, 11-D, 2-D-, and 37-Fails. These results are a good reflection of the terrible history of the Government of Canada's commitment to working with integrity with First Nations people: act and talk like things will be different, but continue on with the same strategy of acknowledging problems, pacifying with investigations and reports, throwing a few crumbs to keep some happy, then ignoring the real issues until it all starts over again. Then there are more commissions, meetings, forums, or strategy sessions to identify the same old problems that have existed since first contact. The Government of Canada is well aware of the things that can result in a meaningful difference in the lives of First Nations people and their relationship with Canada and its people, but chooses to do very little. It has been 15 years since the release of the Royal Commission on Aboriginal People with very little progress and little hope for any more.

Find Out More

Royal Commission on Aboriginal People Report. 1996.
Royal Commission on Aboriginal People at 10 Years: a Report Card. Assembly of First Nations. 2006.

Slavery

Some First Nations were involved in various aspects of slavery before and after the first visitors arrived on our shores. Many refer to these individuals as captives or prisoners of war as they were not captured, held, or treated the way that African people were when enslaved and brought to the Americas. Prior to first contact some Tribes took prisoners from other Tribes during warfare, raids, or to settle debts. From most accounts, these individuals were treated well, but were forced to work within the community and lived on the outskirts of the community. Captives were kept for varying amounts of time depending on the situation. Some were sent home upon trade between Tribes for each other's members who were captured; others were released when a debt was paid by the captive's family or Tribe.

First Nations people's connection to what is commonly thought of as slavery began after the arrival of Europeans. It is estimated that tens of thousands of First Nations people were forced into slavery in North America by colonial Nations. Many were sold or traded into slavery outside of North America into the Caribbean and West Indies either because it was difficult to control them or it was more profitable to sell them there. Others were enslaved during crop season, but then set free for the remainder of the year as the people who enslaved them did not want to feed and care for them when they were not working to make them money. First Nations women were also forcibly taken by settlers to help them learn about and enter into new territories or trade circles. Some Nations or First Nations individuals also participated in the slave trade in order to gain supplies or other things they needed. Reports show that some Tribes were given slaves after signing treaties in the U.S. in the 1800s and some individuals captured and sold or traded other First Nations people into slavery.

First Nations people were also known to help hide Africans who had escaped slavery. The escapees usually travelled along the Underground Railway to potential freedom in the northern U.S. and Canada and on their way came upon First Nations communities who would often help them to hide and travel to other locations, although some remained and married within First Nations communities. This is especially true in the eastern U.S. where there are now many people with both First Nations and African roots.

Find Out More
wikipedia.org
nativewiki.org

Chapter 3
Community Issues

Today's reality for First Nations people includes many challenges, but also immense hope for the future. I truly believe that the strength that our ancestors drew from their cultural and spiritual beliefs helped them to survive the onslaught of actions, policies, and laws that have been heaped upon us since first contact with visitors to this land. The fact that First Nations people survived hundreds of years of concerted effort to subdue us gives me great strength and hope for the future. Despite all of the challenges that I will review in this chapter, it is important to remember that our people have such rich and vibrant histories, traditions, and beliefs to draw from that can help us to overcome anything. Those of us who have chosen to draw upon those strengths have been strengthened. Those who draw upon other healthy ways have been strengthened. Those who are still steeped in their anger, pain, confusion, dependence, self-pity, or shame need to learn about the history, culture, traditions, and strengths of First Nations people as it will strengthen them also.

First Nations people's health has been negatively affected in many ways since we were forced to abandon our traditional lifestyles, which were much more active, included access to healthy food, and did not include many of today's social and economic problems. Our physical health has declined due to a more sedentary life and the introduction of new foods that our bodies cannot easily process such as white flour, sugar, and cow's milk. The many abuses that we have suffered have led to poor mental health including low self-esteem, depression, anxiety, suicidal ideation; a skewed sense of sexuality which has led to sexually transmitted infections, early pregnancy, and to babies being born with health problems; and unhealthy coping mechanism such as violence and addictions. Diabetes, heart disease, obesity, and HIV/AIDS are all growing problems throughout First Nations communities. These are just some of the ways our lives have been negatively affected over the past few centuries.

This chapter includes the most common and general issues that we struggle with today. My intention is not to stereotype First Nations people, rather just to bring to light that all of these issues have been caused by externally imposed actions, policies, and laws. Anyone who understands trauma, mental health, addictions, and counselling in general would quickly agree that most of the social issues that First Nations people face today are due to external forces which have resulted in new unhealthy ways of living and coping. So when you read about these issues, please remember all of the good things that I also talk about in this book as that is our history, reality for some today, and our potential for the future.

Poverty

It never ceases to amaze me how many people believe that First Nations people enjoy at least the same standard of living as the average North American. Anyone who knows our current reality knows that that could not be further from the truth. The Campaign 2000 *Report Card on Child and Family Poverty in Canada: 1989-2009* noted that there had been a slight reduction in poverty in Canada over the previous 20 years; however, 49% of off-reserve First Nations children under the age of six lived in low-income families compared to only 18% for other children. The Canadian Centre for Policy Alternatives (CCPA) reviewed the 1996, 2001 and 2006 Canadian Censuses in their 2010 report *The Income Gap Between Aboriginal Peoples and the Rest of Canada* to see if the income gap has changed over the 10 year period. Their review showed that the gap has narrowed only marginally with the median income for First Nations people being 30% lower than for other Canadians, at an abysmal $18,962 per year. At this rate of change, they project that it will be another 63 years before the gap is eliminated. Lower rates of education and employment continue to contribute to the problem; however, the CCPA notes that even when First Nations people have the same level of education, we consistently earn less no matter where we live. The gap exists even on-reserve where *non-First Nations* people earn 34% more on urban reserves than First Nations people do, and a whopping 88% more on rural reserves than First Nations people do. One glimmer of hope was that those who have a bachelor's degree closed the income gap from $3,382 in 1996 to only $648 by 2006. However, only 8% of First Nations people have a bachelor's degree compared to 22% of other Canadians. The CCPA's review of literature revealed a lack of focus on the causal factors of poverty which include the "decimation of traditional economies, the movement of Aboriginal peoples onto increasingly marginal land and the creation of reserves by the colonial administration. Purported to be a solution, assimilation instead decimated entire cultures that had other value, both economic and non-economic, without improving conditions for the people left in its wake." These factors coupled with strategies imposed on First Nations people without meaningful consultation, ownership, or the ability to plan, develop, and carry out the programs ourselves limit the effectiveness of current educational, training, and employment strategies.

The Assembly of First Nations' (AFN) Make Poverty History Campaign identifies meaningful access to education as a key priority in helping to alleviate the high levels of First Nations poverty. They note that the First Nations young population (60% are under the age of 25) cannot be ignored; otherwise, "First Nations people will remain in poverty for generations to come. The youthful First Nations population represents an opportunity for prosperity, not only for First Nations communities but for all Canadians." The AFN notes that First Nations poverty will cost Canada up to $11 billion per year by 2016 in social costs that could be prevented if First Nations people had meaningful and equal access to education, training, and employment opportunities. Poverty leaves individuals vulnerable to unsafe situations, exploitation, and abuse. It may lead to individuals and families being homeless, having to make a decision to live with someone they might not otherwise, being sexually exploited, or having to earn money through illegal or unsafe activities such as prostitution, theft of food or diapers, selling drugs, or fraud. These are choices of desperation, not greed. While I am heartened that the AFN and the provinces are now talking about alleviating poverty in our communities, I am worried that they are not focusing on the core issues that lead to poverty. They must equally and meaningfully address social issues before there can be long lasting change. Simply providing training and employment opportunities is not enough when unacceptable numbers of First Nations people do not have the personal lifeskills necessary to meaningfully take hold of and make the best of opportunities, no matter how much we want to. Rather than setting some up to fail with a one size fits all plan, there must be alternatives that meet the additional needs of those with lower levels of life skills so they can deal with the multiple stresses that come with functioning in today's fast paced and individually focused economy.

Find Out More

2009 Report Card on Child and Family Poverty in Canada: 1989 – 2009. Campaign 2000. 2009.
Determinants of Development Success in the Native Nations of the United States. Jonathan B. Taylor. Native Nations Institute for Leadership, Management and Policy. Udall Center for Studies in Public Policy. Tucson, Arizona. 2008.
The Harvard Project on American Indian Economic Development. Harvard University, Cambridge, Massachusetts.
Committee chastises treatment of aboriginal children in Canada. Star Phoenix Newspaper. April 27, 2007.
The Income Gap Between Aboriginal Peoples and the Rest of Canada. Canadian Centre for Policy Alternatives. 2010.
From Poverty to Prosperity: Opportunities to Invest in First Nations. Assembly of First Nations. 2007.
Federal Government Funding to First Nations: The Facts, the Myths, and the Way Forward. Assembly of First Nations.
Taking Action for First Nations Post-Secondary Education: Access, Opportunity, and Outcomes Discussion Paper. Assembly of First Nations. 2010.
Health of Inuit, Métis and First Nations Adults Living Off-Reserve in Canada: The Impact of Socio-economic Status on Inequalities in Health. Statistics Canada. June 2010.

Sidebar – Standard of Living?

In 2007, the United Nations listed Canada in the top five on their Human Development Index, but within those numbers is the reality that Canada's First Nations people's standard of living is 78th in the world. Canada has been singled out many times by international human rights bodies, including the United Nations, for the abysmal living conditions of First Nations people which are due to the Government of Canada failing to live up to their treaty and constitutional obligations. Even within Canada, there are many reports that indicate that First Nations people are over-represented in almost every negative social and economic statistic. This dismal reality has led to outcries of support for the Assembly of First Nations' A Call to Action Against First Nations Poverty Plan which was launched in 2007 on Parliament Hill with members of Parliament, senators, representatives from national and international humanitarian organizations, and many others in attendance to show their support.

Housing

Many people believe that First Nations people have unlimited access to free housing; however, what many believe to be free housing is actually a right that is tied to our inherent rights as First Nations people and in partial payment for the millions and millions of acres of land that is no longer ours. Many others believe that the houses that are provided are in good condition; however, the reality is that the rates of poor living conditions, over-crowding, and homelessness are staggering. The root cause for all of these issues is an overall lack of funding to build, repair, or renovate housing for First Nations people both on and off-reserve.

The Assembly of First Nations (AFN) reports that many studies about on-reserve housing have shown that there are ongoing issues that need immediate attention including "severe overcrowding, lack of plumbing, no electricity, poor insulation, toxic mould, substandard construction, and a huge accumulation of units in need of major repair." The National Aboriginal Housing Association (NAHA) which advocates for First Nations people living off-reserve (60% of the First Nations population) asserts that a trust must be set up in order to address the dire need for off-reserve housing. NAHA estimates that the trust must start at a modest $100 million dollars per year and build up to $386 million per year to meet the growing need. In a 2010 speech to the Economic Club of Canada, National Inuit Leader Mary Simon stated that "If governments were to do one thing that would have a domino effect in improving Inuit health, and increasing education rates, it would be to solve the Inuit housing crisis."

Mould has infiltrated most reserve housing due to poor construction of federally sponsored housing, little or no ventilation, cold weather, cooking with steam, a lack of awareness of residents about mould, and a lack of funds within households to do the necessary repairs. The prevalence of mould in our communities has had a devastating and expensive effect both in terms of dollars and health. The late detection and lack of action to remove mould has caused respiratory problems such as asthma and emphysema for many, especially our children. An irreversible and extremely tragic effect of mould has been the death of babies due to respiratory distress that was previously mistaken for Sudden Infant Death Syndrome (SIDS). This problem is so large and affects First Nations people at such a high rate that the Government of Canada had to develop specific guide books for Bands, individuals, and housing providers to help them deal with the problems related to poor housing, including how to identify if mould is in a house, how to fix the problem, and related health concerns. The Government of Canada estimates that it will take up to $100 million just to get a handle on mould; however, they are not prepared to provide that amount to fix the problem. The Long Lake First Nation was not prepared to wait for the federal government to address the issue; rather, they filed a class action suit in December 2009 against the Government of Canada that was certified to proceed. In the meantime, the major national Aboriginal organizations continue to pressure the federal government to fully implement and resource the AFN's National Strategy To Address Mould In First Nation Communities. Most reserve houses are over-crowded due to an overall lack of funding to keep up with the demand for new houses, more or improved infrastructure for things such as sewage systems and electricity, and a lack of suitable land to build on. Over-crowding is known to lead to high levels of stress, increased sickness as household members pass on viruses to each other, individual violence if there are unhealthy coping mechanisms, and children being apprehended by child welfare agencies due to a lack of adequate housing. While there are very good housing programs such as Habitat for Humanity, many are not available to on-reserve communities due to federal regulations, remoteness, and a lack of funding. A new and exciting partnership developed in the summer of 2010 when the AFN held a joint press conference with television's home renovation celebrity Mike Holmes about a joint initiative to help improve housing for First Nations people. Initiatives such as this are inspiring and will help put a small dent in the problem for specific families or communities, but it in no way relieves the federal government of its fiduciary responsibility to fix their past mistakes and to provide adequate housing for First Nations people now.

The issue of on-reserve home ownership has always been a contentious issue. The Government of Canada used to build houses for on-reserve status individuals and families. Now they simply provide the funding and the Band handles it. While some on-reserve members are fortunate enough to personally own some of the limited housing, most houses are owned by the Band and often rented to members. Until recently, a Band member who did not personally own the house and the land could not get a loan to expand to accommodate a growing family or to renovate even if there was a mould problem. There is now the federal First Nations Market Housing Fund to which eligible individuals can apply to have their loans guaranteed by the Band so that they can build or renovate a home. However, many First Nations people living on-reserve are unemployed and/or live in poverty so it is difficult to save for the down payment needed to qualify for a loan or even to afford the loan payments themselves.

<u>Find Out More</u>

First Nations Housing Plan. Assembly of First Nations. 2005.
Aboriginal Women and Homelessness. Native Women's Association of Canada. 2007.
Sheltering Urban Aboriginal Homeless People: Assessment of Situation and Needs. National Association of Friendship Centres and University of Winnipeg. 2007.
First Nations Market Housing Fund. Government of Canada.
Mold Matters: A Resource Guide for First Nations Housing Providers. Canada Mortgage & Housing Corporation.
A Time for Action: A National Plan to Address Aboriginal Housing. National Aboriginal Housing Association. 2009.
Holmes on Reserve Homes

National Inuit Leader Says Canada Should Invoke a Temporary Moratorium on Offshore Oil Drilling in the Arctic Until Specific Environmental Safeguards are in Place. Media Release. Inuit Tapiriitt Kanatami. May 26, 2010.
Matrimonial Real Property Consultations: An Information Kit. Native Women's Association of Canada. 2006.
Matrimonial Real Property: A People's Report. Native Women's Association of Canada. 2006.
Family Homes on Reserves and Matrimonial Interests or Rights Act. Government of Canada. 2010.

Sidebar – Homelessness & Women

Homelessness is growing across Canada and First Nations people are over-represented in all major cities. Poverty, social issues, unemployment, family breakdown, discrimination, and poor government policy all contribute to this problem. Social issues such as addictions, violence, or a lack of lifeskills can lead to unemployment or family breakdown which leads to less household income to pay the rent or to women being forced to leave reserves. In many cases of divorce, the *Indian Act's* matrimonial property provisions result in men gaining rights to property, not women. This archaic and sexist provision forces many women and children to leave their homes as women do not have any legal claim to the house that was once her own. Women are often forced to move off-reserve with their children only to face more challenges in an urban setting. Whether people are forced to leave the reserve for their own safety or leave in hope of finding more opportunity in the city for education, training, or employment, many arrive unprepared and end up struggling to make ends meet, live in poverty, or have no funding or childcare which stops them from going to school, training, or work.

Urbanization

Current statistics show that almost 60% of all First Nations people in Canada live in urban settings. Despite this reality, very little attention is paid to those living off-reserve either by government bodies, the general public, or First Nations political leadership. First Nations individuals have been moving to cities for decades for various reasons that are primarily the result of poor federal policies and laws that have inhibited on-reserve economic development, fostered unhealthy behaviors and dependency through residential schools and other federal policy, introduced male domination, and severely interrupted our traditional forms of governance through the *Indian Act* which severely limited women's participation in decision making. The reality is that we either leave to seek better opportunities to improve our lives or we are forced to leave for our own physical or emotional safety. The main reasons for this mass migration to cities include seeking educational, training, and employment opportunities that are not available on-reserve, to be closer to medical care or family, to escape homophobia, to distance ourselves from unhealthy behaviors or memories, or to escape abusive relationships.

While governments go about working with on-reserve Chiefs and Councils, most First Nations people live in the city. Neither treaties nor the *Constitution* state that we will only have our rights if we live on-reserve or that our needs must be met directly through on-reserve Band Councils. The problem is that neither the government nor our Chiefs are listening to the concerns of off-reserve First Nations people. They may hear us, but they can't be listening; otherwise, there would be meaningful change happening. There wouldn't be so much emphasis on on-reserve issues at the expense of those of us living off-reserve. Urban First Nations people would not be a side note in the conversation and with Chiefs adopting phrases that make it sound like they are truly advocating for our needs. Just saying that they are 'working for First Nations people no matter where they live' is not enough. In this case, actions truly speak louder than words. The Government of Canada has made minimal effort to engage and work with urban First Nations people to ensure that our needs are being met and our rights as First Nations people are being honored. As Calvin Helin notes, most of us are voting with our feet by leaving our First Nations communities. We are tired of waiting for changes that can make our communities a better place to live that would allow us all to be safe and to pursue our social, economic, and cultural dreams. The tide will not turn; we will not be moving to our reserves as many of us do not have Indian status, have never been to our reserves or no longer have family there, have strong roots and our families in the city, or know that there is not enough housing or employment on-reserve. The voices of urban First Nations people were captured in the 2010 *Urban Aboriginal Peoples Study* conducted by the Environics Institute. Many individuals stated that while they may stay connected to their home community, they are not likely to move to their reserves. Despite this over-whelming evidence that the day-to-day lives of First Nations people are connected to urban centers, there has been no meaningful change in federal or provincial policy that reflect this reality. This is ironic considering the federal government's long-term efforts to assimilate us into mainstream society. A true commitment to "assimilating" us must include meaningful opportunities to do well socially, economically, and culturally in the urban environment. It is after all in everyone's best interest to provide meaningful opportunities for First Nations individuals to gain the education, skills, and experience needed to become fully self-sufficient. Some may argue that we must do this ourselves; however, as I've laid out in the beginning of this book and then throughout, First Nations people and communities are facing many social issues that are the direct result of the assimilationist policies that have been forced upon us. This reality calls for a similar effort to help us recover from the onslaught that brought us to where we are today.

The federal government's Urban Aboriginal Strategy

(UAS) which started in 2007 is not so much a strategy as it is a funding source for community activities. As a strategy, it is a dismal failure as the funding is not set up to support the urban off-reserve First Nations leadership to work with community members to develop strategies that will identify and meet their own defined needs. Rather, the UAS is severely under-funded and funds are unfairly distributed as they did not take into account population numbers when they decided how much money was to be allocated to each city, it is only in 13 cities, and its goals were defined by the federal government without meaningful consultation with the urban off-reserve First Nations leadership. The Government of Canada is missing an incredible opportunity to utilize the UAS funds to work with urban First Nations leaders to identify what urban First Nations people's needs and goals are and how to best meet them. The other squandered federal opportunity has been in supporting Friendship Centres which are the heart of the First Nations community in urban areas. The Government of Canada's minimal funding to the National Association of Friendship Centres does little to help ensure that urban First Nations people's needs are being identified, much less met. Funding for Friendship Centres was frozen in 1996, and national pressure from First Nations organizations to lift the freeze has so far been ignored by the federal government.

In 2010, the issue of urbanization again reached the international stage when the United Nations Permanent Forum on Indigenous Peoples' Issues called for the Government of Canada to work in cooperation with urban First Nations organizations and leaders to meet the needs of urban First Nations people. The only level of government that seems to be taking the issue of First Nations urbanization seriously are some cities which have entered into working relationships with urban First Nations leaders to help identify and better meet the needs of First Nations people in their city. Cities with formal relationships with urban First Nations leadership include Edmonton, Toronto, Winnipeg, and Montreal. Some First Nations Bands have negotiated agreements with cities in Saskatchewan and

Manitoba to create new reserves in or adjacent to cities. This is accomplished through the federal Additions to Reserve Policy which requires the Band to purchase property and then apply for federal recognition as a reserve. These urban reserves are being set up in order to provide more opportunities for Bands throughout the province to reach urban markets and to develop new economic opportunities, which if successful, will lead to more employment for their Band members. Some cities, such as Vancouver, already included urban reserves that were designated many decades ago in a Nations' traditional territory.

The migration to urban areas has very important consequences for First Nations individuals who are leaving their family, community, and traditional territory. They often leave behind some things that are essential to them as First Nations people which are not easily found or replaced in urban settings. Some of the greatest losses are separation from extended family and friends, cultural practices, community activities, support systems, connection to the land, and traditional foods. These are often replaced by isolation, culture shock, little or no sense of belonging to a community, little or no support system, extreme poverty, racism, and unhealthy eating habits brought on by poverty and no access to our traditional foods. In addition, many individuals move to urban areas without the education, training, or experience needed to upgrade their education and skills or find and retain sufficient employment. Many do not understand the difficulty of living in the city when they leave the reserve; otherwise, they might not move. Others have no choice but to leave to ensure their safety, because they have lost their home after a relationship break-up, or because they need to be near medical care. This reality leaves many of us at a competitive disadvantage, and therefore at risk of poverty, homelessness, depression, poor health, criminal activity, and many forms of exploitation. In order to make ends meet, feed their children, or to even keep a roof over their heads, some are forced to sell or transports drugs, enter the sex trade, or steal which can entrench them in a cycle that is extremely hard to get out of.

Sidebar – Women's Reality

First Nations women have been moving to cities for the same reasons as men do; however, there are particular problems that primarily affect women, and their children. Family violence, sexual abuse, and divorce all leave women vulnerable and often with no choice but to leave their home. Women often flee unhealthy or unsafe situations as single mothers with little or no education, training, money, or support. In order to feed their children or pay the rent, some women are forced to participate in activities that they would not otherwise. Although no person desires to be a drug dealer or a part of the sex trade, some women are pushed to the point where they feel that this is their only option. These activities often lead to low self-esteem, depression, and substance abuse. These effects can in turn lead to women being unable to adequately care for their children, or themselves. This reality either leaves the children not having their day-to-day needs met, being exploited in any number of ways, and/or being apprehended by the ministry responsible for child welfare.

Find Out More

The Government's Duty to Consult Urban Aboriginal People. National Association of Friendship Centres.

Urban Aboriginal Peoples Study. Environics Institute. 2010.

"Real" Indians and Others: Mixed-Blood Urban Native Peoples and Indigenous Nationhood. Bonita Lawrence. University of Nebraska Press. 2004.

In Their Own Voices: Building Urban Aboriginal Communities. Jim Silver. Fernwood Publishing. 2006.

Edmonton Urban Aboriginal Accord

Toronto Urban Aboriginal Framework

First Steps: Municipal Aboriginal Pathways. City of Winnipeg.

Sexual Exploitation

There is very little formal research about sexual exploitation of First Nations people; however, there are a few frequently cited reports that present sound knowledge from sexually exploited individuals, service providers, and law enforcement agencies. Overall, these reports indicate there is a large over-representation of First Nations female and male adults and children in the sex trade in both urban and rural settings. According to the Urban Native Youth Association's *Full Circle* report, sexual exploitation occurs when pimps, johns, partners, friends, family, or anyone else knowingly profits in any way from someone being forced or coerced into performing sexual acts. This could include "receiving money gained through prostitution, receiving anything else that is paid for with the money that is made through prostitution, or receiving anything that is traded for sex including a place to stay, clothes, food, cigarettes, etc." Save the Children's 2000 report *Sacred Lives: Canadian Aboriginal Children and Youth Speak Out About Sexual Exploitation,* was the first national study that focused specifically on First Nations people. The report lists many of the ways in which First Nations people are forced into situations that are sexually exploitive – both within the sex trade and in their daily lives. These situations include individuals in northern or rural areas without cars who are forced to have sexual relations with someone in order to get a ride home, to the doctor, or to flee an unsafe environment; youth who have no safe or welcoming place to go are exploited by older men who in turn provide what youth need including a place to sleep, food, friendship, or drugs; and many are forced into the sex trade in urban settings out of extreme poverty, involvement with gangs, or addictions.

The Native Women's Association of Canada (NWAC), the Royal Canadian Mounted Police, Amnesty International, and others all draw a direct link to the negative effects of colonization including the residential school experience as contributing factors that make First Nations people vulnerable to sexual exploitation and trafficking. This history has left many First Nations people with low self-esteem, poor coping skills, histories of abuse, addictions, and mental health issues. These existing issues are made far worse by sexual exploitation. Those who are sexually exploited are more likely to use alcohol and drugs to help cope with the ensuing distress, become suicidal, contract and possibly spread a sexually transmitted disease, come into conflict with the law, or lose custody of their children. These compounding effects put them further at risk of exploitation or from ever recovering to lead healthy and safe lives. Most are at risk of being physically and sexually assaulted or even killed. Amnesty International and The Sisters in Spirit Campaign report that over 600 First Nations women have gone missing or have been murdered across Canada. Most of the victims of serial killer Robert Pickton were First Nations women who were stuck in the sex trade and addicted to drugs. The issue of sexual trafficking and exploitation of First Nations people extends across North America and beyond. The Minnesota Indian Women's Resource Center's *Shattered Hearts* report shows a high rate of sexual trafficking of First Nations females in Minnesota. They note that the Minnesota Human Trafficking Task Force estimated that at least 345 First Nations women and girls had been sexually trafficked between 2005 and 2008. For First Nations people this is literally a life and death issue that must be addressed at all levels both within and outside of the First Nations community.

In order to stop the devastating reality of sexual exploitation, governments and others must do more to help First Nations families and communities recover from the many negative effects of the assimilation process. A federal apology will never be enough if the day-to-day realities for First Nations people do not change. Those who are interested in helping to create positive change can look to reports such as *Sacred Lives* and *Full Circle* as both provide many recommendations that can help to prevent individuals from being sexually exploited, and about how to support those who are attempting to or have left the sex trade.

Find Out More

Sacred Lives: Canadian Aboriginal Children and Youth Speak Out About Sexual Exploitation. Cherry Kingsley and Melanie Mark. Save the Children Canada. 2000.
Full Circle. Lynda Gray and Melanie Mark. Urban Native Youth Association. 2002.
Shattered Hearts: The Commercial Sexual Exploitation Of American Indian Women And Girls. Minnesota Indian Women's Resource Center. 2009.
"Domestic Sex Trafficking of Aboriginal Girls in Canada: Issues and Implications." First Peoples Child and Family Review No. 3: 57-71. Sethi, Anupriya. 2009.

Friendship Centres

The development of what became known as Friendship Centres began in the 1950s when many First Nations people began migrating to urban settings to pursue better opportunities, fulfill their dreams, or find a safer life. Toronto, Winnipeg, and Vancouver were a few of the first cities where Friendship Centres developed. These early volunteer-run agencies served a number of important purposes: they offered a place for the first waves of First Nations people to find and gather with their peers, offered what programs and services they could with the little, if any, funding they received, were a referral agency, and built a network of supports with other organizations through their advocacy work. The types and number of supports that Friendship Centres wanted and needed to offer began to grow as more First Nations people arrived in cities and their needs expanded. By 1968, there were 26 Friendship Centres across the country, each struggling to survive without core funding or an organized body to advocate on their behalf. In 1969, a steering committee was struck to determine if there was a need for a national organization to represent Friendship Centres in their efforts to secure federal funding and create a unified voice for urban First Nations people. These efforts resulted in the establishment of the National Association of Friendship Centres (NAFC) in 1972. Around the same time, the Government of Canada established the Migrating Native Peoples Program (now called the Aboriginal Friendship Centres Program) which would provide financial support to Friendship Centres. In 1996, administrative responsibility for this program was transferred out of government hands to the NAFC along with the transfer of authority. However, it also came with a freeze on funding which has yet to be lifted despite the proven needs of urban First Nations people by the NAFC.

While some people may question the need for Friendship Centres and view them as a way for First Nations people to segregate themselves, most First Nations people recognize their importance. Some of us do well in any setting, while others prefer to go only to Friendship Centres for various reasons, just as Italian, Portuguese, or Chinese people like to go to their cultural centres. The important thing is that we all need somewhere to belong. The Government of Canada notes that Friendship Centres provide "a wide range of culturally appropriate programs and services directed at improving the lives and strengthening the cultural identity of urban Aboriginal people." This statement is validated by the NAFC's estimate of almost one million visits to Friendship Centres in 2010 alone.

The Institute on Governance's 2008 evaluation of Friendship Centres reported that there are six common threads of a successful Friendship Centre: 1) they have both strong leadership and a strong board; 2) they have a clear strategic plan and evaluation processes that are regularized, ongoing, and followed-up on; 3) they have formal structures that are adhered to, but that also allow a degree of flexibility to respond to emerging needs and trends; 4) they effectively manage their dual role of service delivery and advocacy; 5) their structures, policies, and working atmosphere are based on First Nations values such as transparency, accountability, respect, and client-based service, inclusion of youth and Elders, and they see the First Nations community as both client and advisor, and the board of directors and staff view themselves as members of that same community; 6) they actively seek new funding, diversify their funding sources, and have shown entrepreneurial success.

In 2009, the NAFC represented 118 Friendship Centres across Canada, of which most were not-for-profit organizations that were governed by an elected Board of Directors. The NAFC notes that their member organizations employ over 2,100 people and provide programs and services in the areas of "culture, family, youth, sports and recreation, language, justice, housing, health, education, employment, economic development and …a variety of miscellaneous projects ranging from soup kitchens and food banks to administration and operational activities." While 99 of the 118 Friendship Centres receive core funding, that funding is not adequate. The NAFC reports that in 2009 the national average amount needed to operate a Friendship Centre was $358,997, while the average core funding they could provide to Centres was only $129,009 (i.e. only 36% of what is needed to operate effectively). This massive shortfall results in staff spending large amounts of time fundraising, proposal writing, and recruiting and training volunteers rather than directly serving the community. Their dedicated efforts supplement the meagre yearly federal allocation of $16.1 million to the NAFC for all Friendship Centres. The NAFC reported that in 2009, Friendship Centres were able to secure additional funding from non-federal government sources of $124 million to hire staff and provide important programs and services. The Government of Canada commits funding to the NAFC in five year cycles. The NAFC was greatly disappointed when in 2009 its mandate was renewed without any increase of funding despite the last increase having been in 1996 and despite the reality that almost 60% of First Nations people now live in cities.

Find Out More

Friendship Centre Movement: Best Practices in Governance and Management. J. Graham & M. Kinmond. Institute on Governance. 2008.

The State of the Friendship Centre Movement: 2009. National Association of Friendship Centres. 2009.

Urban Aboriginal Economic Development: A Friendship Centre Perspective. National Association of Friendship Centres. 2009.

Downtown Eastside & Inner City Issues

The most visible indication of First Nations people's pain and suffering can be seen on the streets of most inner city neighbourhoods, especially in the Downtown Eastside of Vancouver, B.C. This is where our brothers and sisters languish in their pain and/or find a place of belonging without judgement. Many of these people are the individuals with heavy addictions, who are suffering beyond what they can or want to face, are isolated from their family and community, or have lost hope. This is true for all people, not just First Nations people, but we are over-represented in these visible areas of the city that most readily reflect what is wrong with North American society. This is not to say that all people who live in the inner cities have addictions issues, do not have a support system, or have lost hope. If you talk to the right people, you will be envious of the sense of community and caring that exists in the shadows of the more blatant and visible street activities that dominate everyone's external views.

While some will say that the Downtown Eastside has plenty of services, there is not enough of some things such as housing, daycare, or addictions services. There is little understanding of just how huge this problem is; there are literally thousands of people in less than a 10 block area. If the average person on the streets of the Downtown Eastside were in a well-enough or strong-enough position to seek the assistance they need, they would not be on the streets. Many have over-whelming addiction issues, have lost trust in people, have suffered too much pain and loss, or do not have the resilience, will, support, or skills needed to overcome their struggles. Despite the types or number of services available, services must be relevant and welcoming before enough trust can be built to encourage people to even enter their doors to seek something new.

Rather than allowing our governments to maintain these dumping grounds, we need to ask why there is so little being doing to help everyone who needs support to prevent them from ever winding up on the streets. In this day and age when there is so much more understanding of and emphasis on how important it is to take care of our emotional and mental health, there is no excuse for our governments to almost completely ignore this reality. Even Oprah Winfrey has highlighted this reality for millions of people across North America, which is more than our governments have done. We now know that many of our health issues, weight gain, job loss, family violence, sexual exploitation and abuse, and other social issues are directly connected to our mental and emotional health which has most often been affected by traumatic experiences. Despite this knowledge, governments continue to worry about the next election rather than the next generation of people who will continue to face the same problems that their parents did because they are not offered meaningful and safe opportunities to work towards changing their lives.

Gangs – A Place to Belong

First Nations gangs are on the rise in major cities, rural communities, and reserves across the country. There are very few reports focusing on First Nations gang involvement and even less current data. The 2002 *Canadian Police Survey on Youth Gangs* reports that 22% of the estimated 7,000+ youth gang members were First Nations. This survey and Dr. Mark Totten's work both indicate that most First Nations gangs consist largely of youth and are usually homogenous, and that many youth are recruited in prison. Recent articles note that First Nations gangs range from disorganized to highly organized, but rarely are they at the same level as other organized gangs that reach into jails to recruit, have definite hierarchies, and are enduring. First Nations gangs are most prevalent in the prairie provinces including major cities such as Edmonton, Saskatoon, Winnipeg, and Regina. They often use names that are connected to their First Nations heritage such as the Warriors, Red Alert, Native Syndicate and the Indian Posse. Like other gangs, First Nations gangs vary in their level of violence, drug trafficking, prostituting of young women, and recruitment strategies.

Most reports on gangs conclude that poor social and economic conditions, inter-generational problems brought on by assimilationist policies, family breakdown, racism, high levels of incarceration, and social exclusion all leave First Nations youth vulnerable to gang recruitment. Dr. Martin Brokenleg, a leader in the area of youth empowerment work, believes that because First Nations youth are forced to live in a bi-cultural world they must be able to form a strong bi-cultural identity to thrive in it rather than letting racism or cultural differences lead to social segregation. He notes that gangs fill a void in youth's lives when they lack a positive place within their family, peer group, or community. This lack of belonging, as highlighted in the Circle of Courage Model Dr. Brokenleg co-developed, leaves youth vulnerable to gang recruitment as gangs are skilled at making youth feel like they are special, needed, and belong at a time in their adolescence when belonging is crucial to their personal identity formation. The lack of belonging was referred to recently by the head of the RCMP National Aboriginal Policing Services' Aboriginal Gang File who stated that "Aboriginal youth are just wanting to belong to somebody." The Native Women's Association of Canada noted that "gangs may offer these youth a sense of belonging, recognition and self-esteem as they are establishing their personal identity and networks."

Many point to First Nations culture and traditions as the basis of healing, increased self-pride, and creating a sense of belonging to prevent gang involvement or to help youth exit gangs. Dr. Mark Totten, an expert in the area of Aboriginal gangs, identifies the Prince Albert Warrior Spirit Walking Project, the Regina Anti-Gang Service (RAGS) Project, and Vancouver's CHARM Program (now known as Eastside Space for Aboriginal Youth – EASY Project) as promising practices for reducing gang involvement as these projects are culturally competent, have gender-specific responses, and let youth know that they are cared for by providing wrap-around services late into the night. Dr. Totten notes that many of the programs he is evaluating that are showing promising results are based on the Circle of Courage Model which focuses on four key areas: belonging, independence, mastery, and generosity. It is also likely that the decline of traditional rights of passage ceremonies that helped to acknowledge and support individuals through significant life transitions such as puberty has left many First Nations youth vulnerable to the unhealthy options that gangs can offer.

There is still lots of work to be done in this area to identify the actual number of youth who are being recruited into gangs, ways for communities to recognize signs of gang formation, and what types of interventions work to prevent gang involvement or to encourage and help youth to exit gang life. A stronger focus on these areas along with health and healing strategies for First Nations people overall may help to reduce the loss of First Nations youth to gangs.

Find Out More

Reclaiming Youth at Risk: Our Hope for the Future. Larry K. Brendtro, Martin Brokenleg and Steve Van Bockern. National Educational Service. 2001.

Aboriginal Youth Gangs: Preventative Approaches. J.P. Preston, S. Carr-Stewart and C. Northwest. First Peoples Child & Family Review. Vol. 4, No. 2, p. 152-160. 2009.

Preventing Aboriginal Youth Gang Involvement in Canada: A Gendered Approach. Mark Totten. Paper Prepared for Aboriginal Policy Research Conference. March 2009.

Aboriginal Women and Gangs An Issue Paper. National Aboriginal Women's Summit. June 20-22, 2007.

Addictions

One of the most visible signs that First Nations people are still experiencing the inter-generational effects of the residential school experience is the prevalence of addictions – alcohol, drugs, food, and gambling - which includes bingo. The Canadian Centre on Substance Abuse, the Aboriginal Healing Foundation, Dr. Gabor Maté, and National Native Alcohol and Drug Abuse Program are a few of the many experts who identify addictions as a coping mechanism for First Nations people who have experienced inter-generational trauma from residential schools and residual effects of poverty, racism, and poor social conditions. Although there are no definitive studies on the rate of addictions within First Nations communities, many refer to the 2002-2003 First Nations Regional Longitudinal Health Survey which notes that the number of First Nations people who *do not drink at all* (44%) is more than double the overall population rate of only 17.8%. However, the number of heavy or binge drinkers is higher in the First Nations community than the overall population. In *Fighting Firewater Fictions,* Richard Thatcher asserts that First Nations binge and long-term drinking are linked to a 'drinking style' that is similar to that of young people who drink fast and hard to get drunk with few inhibitions such as worrying about the loss of employment, family, or reputation that would stop them. He believes that First Nations people learned this from early contact with fur traders, miners, and others who also had this style of drinking. Mr. Thatcher believes that today, many First Nations people do not have the same social advantages, such as access to education and training, that others do so they do not reach a stage in life that would give them a reason to leave the young partying stage of life. In fact, Mr. Thatcher believes that the lack of opportunity also contributes to the continuation of drinking as a sense of hopelessness sets in. Radio host, writer, actor, and comedian Darrel Dennis notes that while the Irish are celebrated for their supposed heavy drinking, the opposite is true for First Nations people. This difference may be due to the added problems of homelessness and poverty that lead to First Nations people being more visible living on the street and walking or bussing home.

> *"Traditional teachings counter the residential school legacy by replacing the shame-based beliefs that children were taught about Aboriginal cultures with beliefs that are life-sustaining ... many cultural practices are also tools for restoring healthy, respectful relationships."*
> Addictive Behaviours Among Aboriginal People in Canada. Aboriginal Healing Foundation.

Today, First Nations people suffer from the same addictions that mainstream society does. Alcohol, drugs, and gambling are blatant signs of underlying problems, but food addiction is one of the least known or understood problems in our community. There are plenty of experts who have written about the consumption of high carbohydrate food as a coping mechanism for those who have experienced trauma and loss. The Oprah Winfrey Show has brought this message to millions of people, but most people still struggle to overcome this problem until they can deal with their underlying emotional issues. Many of us use food as a coping strategy without even being aware of it. I now recognize that I used to run to a fast food restaurant when I was stressed or angry. The carbs would calm me down, but only temporarily just like street drugs would if I used them. The more we are exposed to this information, the more likely we are to acknowledge, understand, and do something about it. Rarely do I hear anyone in our community talk about it. Hopefully, this little call to action will encourage our health professionals, counsellors, leaders, and others to pay more attention and work towards having food addiction officially recognized as a problem that we need to address when working with our people, especially given the rates of obesity, heart problems, and diabetes that are plaguing our communities.

There are many ways that First Nations communities are addressing the problem of addictions, from offering programs, educating people about the underlying issues that lead to addictive behaviors, helping to revive traditional teachings and practices, and banning alcohol and drugs from a community. The Moose Cree First Nation, Wikwemikong Unceded Indian Reserve, Aamjiwnaang First Nation, and Natuashish have all implemented this strategy at some point. RCMP Sgt. Ren Osmond reported that since the ban on alcohol and drugs in these communities, the number of assaults went down by at least 40% and the number of people being sent to jail was down by 50%.

Find Out More

Addictive Behaviours Among Aboriginal People in Canada. Aboriginal Healing Foundation. 2007.
Fetal Alcohol Syndrome Among Aboriginal People in Canada: Review and Analysis of the Inter-generational Links to Residential Schools. Caroline L. Tait. Aboriginal Healing Foundation. 2003.
Canadian Centre on Substance Abuse
Fighting Firewater Fictions: Moving Beyond the Disease Model of Alcoholism in First Nations. Richard W. Thatcher. University of Toronto Press. 2004.
In the Realm of Hungry Ghosts: Close Encounters With Addiction. Dr. Gabor Maté. 2009.
Traveller Newsletter, Issue 7. National Native Addictions Partnership Foundation. 2009.

Rant – Gambling

Sure gambling is a personal choice, but what if you don't have the lifeskills to control unhealthy urges? I understand that casinos and bingo bring money and jobs into First Nations communities, but they also feed people's addictions. So while there are some benefits to those communities that use their profits for community development or personal healing programs, the people who already have unhealthy coping mechanisms are going to have more ways to self-destruct. Our communities could choose to take a stronger stance than mainstream governments do when it comes to problem gamblers. We could ban chronic gamblers from our casinos if we wanted to, if we really meant that the casino is there for the betterment of the community. It's time for our leaders to walk the walk on this issue, not just talk the talk. We cannot afford to prosper from the misery of others, especially within our own community. So unless leaders can guarantee that all profits will go towards healing programs, cultural camps, and other healthy community building activities, I believe casinos should not be allowed in our communities.

Violence

Violence is prevalent throughout North America, and the First Nations community is no exception. According to the General Social Survey on Victimization (GSSV) report, in 2009 12% of First Nations people over the age of 14 reported having been a victim of a sexual assault, robbery or physical assault committed by someone other than a spouse or common-law partner, which is more than double the rate among non-First Nations people (5%). First Nations people were three times more likely to report being sexually assaulted and twice as likely to report being physically assaulted than non-First Nations people. We continue to experience violence by non-First Nations people with high rates of hate crimes going unreported; our young athletes continue to be both verbally and physically assaulted on their sports playing fields and in locker rooms; our women are abused, raped, and murdered; and our children and youth are sexually assaulted and attacked simply for being who they are. The Native Women's Association of Canada (NWAC) has been successful at raising awareness of the almost 600 missing and murdered First Nations women across Canada. Our women continue to be brutalized and murdered without the justice system paying much attention. Until all levels of government send a strong message that this is unacceptable, our daughters, sisters, aunts, nieces, mothers, and grandmothers will continue to suffer needlessly.

Justice Canada reports show that much of the violence against First Nations people is committed by First Nations people. Even after we account for the under-reporting, disbelief by authorities of those who report being a victim of a violent crime, and less-than-adequate investigation by police, we are still left with the simple fact that we are facing high rates of violence within our own communities. Physical, mental, and emotional violence that were learned in residential schools have been passed on through the generations as extremely unhealthy ways of dealing with anger, frustration, confusion, and shame.

The issue is further magnified by the loss of healthy coping and communication skills and the introduction of using alcohol and drugs as coping mechanisms. The GSSV noted that crimes involving a First Nations victim (67%) were more likely to include alcohol or illegal drug use by the perpetrator than crimes with a non-First Nations victim (52%). This does not mean that all our communities have high rates of violence or that we are a naturally violent people; it means that some of us are exhibiting unhealthy violent behaviors as a way to deal with things that we are unwilling or unable to recognize, acknowledge, or address in a healthy way. We need to heal from our individual and collective past and relearn the skills needed to deal with anger, shame, confusion, and frustration in healthy ways. I have nothing but faith that we are a peaceful and spiritual people by nature, but we must face our reality now so that we can return to being a community that takes care of each other rather than hurts each other. Prior to colonization, our communities had very strict rules regarding abuse of another person, so there was likely very little of the type of abuses that we see today. This reality needs to be shared throughout our community so that people realize that this is not an acceptable way to live, and then each person can change their own behaviors.

The GSSV reported that First Nations women were three times more likely than non-First Nations women to report being a victim of spousal violence in the previous five years and they were more likely to report that they had feared for their life as a result of the violence. Violence against women within the First Nations community is not a subject that is generally openly talked about or acknowledged in First Nations communities unless it is in reaction to a specific incident or to do with the missing and murdered women across the country. Simply put, silence is literally killing us. It does absolutely no one any good to ignore violence. We cannot afford to let the shame of the social problems in our community hold us back from changing for the better. I am not ashamed or afraid to openly state that there are varying rates of violence in our community that ranges from abused children, beaten wives, harassed and beaten Two-spirit individuals, abused Elders, emotionally battering, and sexually assaulted children, youth, and adults. To give in to shame is to abandon the hope that our community can do better. I am not willing to do that.

Actions taken and work done by groups such as NWAC and the Ontario Native Women's Association in partnership with the Ontario Federation of Indian Friendship Centres are beginning to take hold and their tireless efforts have led to some men starting to take leadership roles on this issue. Important steps in reversing this problem are also beginning to happen on a broader scale throughout our communities. Many are learning how inter-generational trauma is negatively affecting our families. With this knowledge, many are realizing that they can have a better life that is free from violence. A very important step has been acknowledging that those who are violent also need support so that they can change their behavior. This has opened the door for them to change without being shamed. Everyone in the family is affected by violence within families, but the main perpetrators are men. Although this is true, I understand that these men most likely suffered from violence as children so they were taught how to behave this way. This is in no way an excuse, only a reminder that perpetrators of violence are sometimes victims too, and need the proper supports to help them replace these destructive behaviours with healthy ones before they pass it on to future generations. There are some groups that are offering men safe, accessible, and culturally appropriate services and are helping men to identify the root causes of their violent behavior. Other groups also include partners when appropriate and safe. Most groups provide information that helps participants to understand the history that has led them and their communities to this situation and many also include cultural practices that help create a sense of safety and belonging. These two strategies are helping those who are violent, and their partners, to open up to change, which includes healthy communication to help them overcome the shame, anger, and loss that have resulted from the abuse.

Thankfully, there has been more acknowledgement of this issue in our communities and groups are doing good work to bring this issue to light. Groups and organizations are working together through initiatives such as the National Aboriginal Circle Against Family Violence which offers training, newletters, and advocacy, and acts as a coordinating body to advocate for more First Nations anti-violence programs. People at the grassroots level are also taking action. In 2006, a group of Native women cycled across Canada to raise awareness about violence against women; in Vancouver, the Warriors Against Violence Program is incorporating culture and history to help men, women and youth address the violence that is affecting their lives; the Native Youth Sexual Health Network gathered stories from First Nations men to get their input into helping to end violence against women; and the Saugeen First Nation hosted a Take Back the Night and Sister in Spirit Walk to engage community members in bringing the issue of violence out in to the open. This multi-level and diverse approach will help to bring about change, especially as more of us join them.

Find Out More

Warrior-Caregivers: Understanding the Challenges and Healing of First Nations Men. W. J. (Bill) Mussell. Aboriginal Healing Foundation. 2005.
Addressing Violence Against Aboriginal Women, the Elderly, and Children: A Policy Paper. Native Women's Association of Canada. 2008.
Missing Sisters Awareness Walk
Aboriginal Elder Abuse in Canada. Claudette Dumont-Smith. Aboriginal Healing Foundation. 2002.
A Strategic Framework to End Violence Against Aboriginal Women. Ontario Native Women's Association & Ontario Federation of Indian Friendship Centres. 2007.
Warriors Against Violence Society. Vancouver, B.C.

Kizhaay Anishinaabe Niin: I am a Kind Man: Tool Kit for Action, Community Action Kit to Encourage Aboriginal Youth and Men to Speak out Against Violence Towards Women. Ontario Federation of Indian Friendship Centres. 2006.
Violent Victimization of Aboriginal People in the Provinces, 2009. Statistics Canada Juristat Report. March 11, 2011.
Native Women's Association of Canada
Protecting the Circle: Aboriginal Men Ending Violence Against Women. Native Youth Sexual Health Network. 2010.
Aboriginal Domestic Violence in Canada. Four Worlds Centre for Development Learning. Aboriginal Healing Foundation. 2003.
Call Into the Night: An Overview of Violence Against Aboriginal Women (Interim Report). Standing Committee on the Status of Women. 2011.

Feminism

First Nations communities have changed significantly over the past few hundred years with the introduction of patriarchal systems. When coupled with social problems, this has significantly changed our communities for the worse. First Nations Elders and other historians note that most First Nations communities were what many refer to as egalitarian (i.e. classless, free, or open). While communities may have had a Chieftainship or other perceived forms of hierarchy, most worked together for the good of the community. Chiefs and Matriarchs worked in the best interest the people, not themselves or their personal beliefs. Women continue to be the backbone of our communities, but today our communities are primarily represented by men in *Indian Act* Band politics and First Nations political movements, in public settings, and in our First Nations forms of governance.

Although women continue to suffer under this new system, very few embrace mainstream feminism as a means of helping our communities return to being more inclusive and respectful. Two important collections of First Nations women's writing, *Making Space for Indigenous Feminism* and *Indigenous Women and Feminism: Politics, Activism, Culture,* have begun the movement to fill the large gap in published First Nations feminist literature. Many of the authors believe that mainstream feminism is not the best vehicle to help First Nations women address their unique issues and concerns. They note that mainstream feminism is overly focused on white middle class women's issues, despite claims that it is working in the interest of all women. While First Nations women, along with women of color, did make some inroads in the second and third wave of feminism, it has not been in any significant manner that has either helped to change their own lives or mainstream feminism. Many First Nations women involved in mainstream feminist movements or groups have found that they had to fight to gain any attention to their unique issues as First Nations women. Many of the contributors to the two collections acknowledge the benefits of feminist actions and movements, but most believe that there must be an Indigenous feminist movement. Indigenous-focused feminism would better reflect our shared colonial history and ensuing imposition of patriarchal and colonial systems in our lives and communities. Most First Nations women are not worried about ensuring that women have the same rights as men; rather, the focus is on working together on our collective empowerment and healing. Many believe that a return to our traditional forms of community and governance can eventually lead to everyone being treated equally again, not just women.

You will find some First Nations women who publicly declare themselves as feminists, but more often than not, many First Nations women who are feminists do not. Many do not declare themselves as feminists as they fear being marginalized and harassed in some areas of the First Nations community. Others have similar beliefs as feminists or behave in ways which are commonly considered feminist, but they will not join feminist groups or speak out as a declared feminist. Rather, they feel more included, safer, and more effective if they simply speak from their worldview as First Nations women.

> *"Those who struggle for gender equality are often seen, sometimes erroneously, as opposing traditional Indigenous practices and forms of social organization. Thus, Indigenous feminism frequently elicits accusations that it fractures communities and undermines more pressing struggles for Indigenous autonomy."*
>
> Indigenous Women and Feminism: Politics, Activism, Culture

Well-known First Nations women such as Lee Maracle, the late Patricia Monture, Sharon McIvor, Sandy Grande, Andrea Smith, and many others have consistently worked to restore First Nations women to their inherent and rightful role as leaders in First Nations communities. Their work in classrooms,

Band offices, community gatherings, the courts, and many other venues has led the way in raising the profile of First Nations women's realities and unique needs. Without these strong and giving women, individuals such as myself would not have the strength to fight against oppressive systems that continue to marginalize First Nations women.

I believe that in most First Nations communities, there was a more equal valuing of people, where everyone was cared for, had rights and responsibilities, and had gifts that were special. For those who are sceptical, you can just look to many of the phrases and words that our public speakers still use today. Most talk about responsibilities to the community as a whole, respect for our Elders and ancestors, women being the culture bearers and backbone of our community, that it takes a whole community to raise a child, and many other wonderful things that have become aspirations rather than realities in most communities. It is because of this reality that First Nations women are forced to fight for women-specific rights otherwise they may be excluded from the community altogether through things such as Bill C-31, matrimonial property rights, or family violence.

I applaud many of the efforts of feminists as I believe in this modern world we need to incorporate as much information and action as possible to address issues that disproportionately affect women in any community. Despite all of this, the concept of declaring myself as a feminist is so far from my consciousness that I did not at first even consider it as a subject for this book. I have plenty of information and thoughts about our women's issues and concerns, but I don't feel the need to label this as feminist thinking.

Find Out More

Making Space for Indigenous Feminism. Joyce Green, editor. Fernwood Publishing. 2007.
Red Pedagogy. Sandy Grande. Rowman & Littlefield. 2004.
Indigenous Women and Feminism: Politics, Activism, Culture.

C. Suzack, S.M. Huhndorf, J. Perreault, and J. Barman editors. UBC Press. 2010.

Being Again of One Mind: Oneida Women and the Struggle for Decolonization. Lina Sunseri. UBC Press. 2010.

Employment

> *"If Aboriginal Canadians were, by 2017, able to increase their level of educational attainment to the level of non-Aboriginal Canadians in 2001, the average annual GDP growth rate in Canada would be up to 0.036 percentage point higher, or an additional cumulative $71 billion (2001 dollars) over the 2001-2017 period" and if the employment and unemployment gap were closed the amount would increase to $160 billion."*
>
> Centre for the Study of Living Standards

The World Health Organization, the United Nations, the Government of Canada, and many others list education and employment as two of the key social determinants of good health, especially in relation to relieving poverty and its accompanying psychological and social issues. Statistics Canada, the Assembly of First Nations, the Centre for the Study of Living Standards, and other experts note that there needs to be a continued increase of educational attainment for First Nations people before there will be a meaningful and sustained increase in employment rates, especially for youth.

The employment rate for First Nations people has risen over the past few decades with more individuals completing their education or starting their own business. However, while the numbers are encouraging, they do not tell the whole story. When viewing employment numbers one must remember they include temporary and part-time employment, not just full time or permanent employment and the unemployment numbers are not measured against the entire population. Rather, they only include those who are working, anticipating a return to work within four weeks, and those who are available for or looking for work. In addition, employment numbers do not indicate the level of pay for those jobs. So please be careful when reading any numbers related to employment or unemployment as they cannot tell the entire story. The greatest stimulus for First Nations employment continues to be access to meaningful education opportunties.

Overall Employment Numbers

In 2006, First Nations individuals who had not finished high school had an overall employment rate of only 47% (broken down to on-reserve 37% , Indian status off-reserve 46%, without Indian status off-reserve 56%, Inuit 49%, and for Métis 59%). The addition of a university education shot the employment rate up to 80% which is comparable to non-First Nations people, however only 8% of First Nations people had attained university education which is less than one-third the non-First Nations average of 25%.

Off-Reserve Employment Numbers

The 2009, employment rate for off-reserve First Nations people ages 25-64 was 57.0%, compared to 61.8% for non-First Nations people, with most individuals working in health care, social assistance, trade, construction and manufacturing. The 2008-09 economic downturn resulted in more off-reserve First Nations people losing their jobs than non-First Nations people resulting in the gap in employment rates widening from 3.5 percentage points in 2008 to 4.8 percentage points in 2009; for First Nations youth aged 15-24 their employment rate fell by 6.8 percentage points compared to 4.2 percentage points for non-First Nations youth.

The unemployment rate was especially hard for First Nations people during the recent economic downturn as it rose from 10.4% in 2008 to 13.9% in 2009, which is much higher than the non-First Nations number which only rose two points from 6.0% to 8.1%.

Entrepreneurs

One area that is showing great promise is First Nations

entrepreneurship. First Nations individuals are clearly taking their destiny into their own hands by creating opportunities for themselves. The Canadian Council for Aboriginal Business' *Promise and Prosperity: The Aboriginal Business Survey* reports that First Nations entrepreneurship and business ownership grew by 38% from 27,000 in 2001 to 37,000 in 2006 which was five times the national growth rate. The majority (61%) of First Nations businesses are prosperous, stable, and growing. Eighty-one percent of these entrepreneurs consider the lack of access to financing or lack of access to equity or capital as the greatest barriers to success for First Nations entrepreneurs.

Employment & Economic Development Opportunities

In many cases, First Nations people's access to employment is greatly limited due to our place of residence. Many First Nations reserves are in remote locations, do not offer a realistic commuting time or costs to get to jobs in areas outside of our communities, or do not have many education, training, or employment opportunities. Our employment rates are also lower than non-First Nations people due to the social issues that many of us face due to the lingering effects of bad government policy. This has left some people unready to adequately train for, find, or retain meaningful employment regardless of where they live.

Some might believe that because First Nations people have reserves they can start their own business in logging, mining, fishing, or other economic activities. However, the reality is that First Nations people do not own the reserve land or have the autonomy to extract resources from their community in most cases. Even if a First Nations Band has the right to harvest natural resources such as fish, wood, minerals, or oil, they often do not have the financial capital or credit to capitalize on these opportunities to create jobs in their communities. This often leaves them at the mercy of large corporations that are able to exploit First Nation's lack of opportunity for their own benefit by negotiating unfair terms because they know the First Nations has very little options to create economic opportunities in their community. Some agreements include promises of jobs for First Nations people; others have profit sharing; but most result in very little profit for First Nations communities.

Find Out More

The Potential Contribution of Aboriginal Canadians to Labour Force, Employment, Productivity and Output Growth in Canada, 2001-2017. Centre for the Study of Living Standards. 2007.
Canadian Council for Aboriginal Business: Aboriginal Business Survey. 2011.
2006 Canadian Census. Statistics Canada.

Culture – What's the Big Deal?

First Nations people have suffered tremendous cultural loss and disruption due to assimilation efforts that sought to completely change our way of life so that we would become different people. Well we did become different people, just not the people who governments were hoping for. Instead of being assimilated individuals who fit seamlessly into mainstream society and values, we are a mere shell of our former cultural selves faced with many social ills brought on by those same assimilation efforts. Governments hate that they have to deal with the social problems we face today, yet the irony is that the very cultures that they so vigorously sought to destroy are exactly what we need to help us recover from the 500 years of externally imposed hardship. Anyone who has not been exposed to or learned about their own specific cultural teachings, beliefs, or practices might not understand the significance of culture to an individual or community. That's okay, not everyone needs to understand the importance of our cultures to us. We just need those who purposefully stand in the way of our regaining and practicing our culture and traditions to move aside so that we can regain what has always been, and will always be, our own ways of living.

First Nations cultures that were purposefully disrupted and damaged are extremely valuable to us as individuals and sustained our ancestors in healthy communities since the beginning of time. Our cultures defined who we were as individuals and in relation to others, taught us our roles and responsibilities, instilled values, gave us purpose, and taught us to be thankful to the Creator and for all living things. Those of us who have not been exposed to our true culture, or are just learning about it, have missed out on so much. I cannot deny my anger at being denied the opportunity to be raised within my own culture; yet I have such happiness that I am learning about it now. I can only dream about how much of a stronger, healthier, and confident person I would be if I was immersed in

Tsimshian culture which is based on a strong connection to the Creator and our ancestors, respect for every living being and the earth, extended families, and strong communities. Those are the important things that I have been denied access to, even to this day as we struggle to find our way back to the ways of our ancestors. For various reasons not every First Nations person will find culture meaningful for them. There are those who have checked it out, but have decided that it is not that important to them; others have chosen to stay away as they are unwilling to be a part of what they perceive to be an unhealthy community or they have internalized the racism that was forced upon them.

Today, many First Nations people are struggling to overcome our collective history of assimilationist policies that have not only introduced negative behaviours into our lives, but also took away our cultural traditions that could help us to recover from the traumas that we continue to experience as a result of the inter-generational effects of the residential school experience and other assimilationist policies. Healing ceremonies, healthy families, spirituality, and self-pride as First Nations people are just a few of the things that were damaged that could have helped us to recover from traumatic events rather than passing it down to our children. Over the last few decades, many First Nations people have been relearning the traditions of our ancestors. It is giving them a sense of belonging, acceptance, pride, and strength. Young people who are being exposed to canoe journeys and the accompanying traditional protocols are returning with their heads held higher and with a stronger sense of pride in themselves as a First Nations person. I remember in 1998 when my children and I were first exposed firsthand to our Tsimshian culture, stories, songs, and dances. What a sense of belonging and fulfillment it evoked in us! I will always honor the positive effect that it has had on my children's lives, as well as mine. They learned so much more about being a First Nations person than I was able to provide. In fact, we learned together what it means to be a First Nations person beyond how we look. We gained a strong sense of belonging to something bigger than themselves, respect, honor, and responsibility. All of these teachings have helped us to become strong, healthy, and positive members of our community. Where sports teams and pop culture used to fill the void, now there is meaningful cultural knowledge that has provided me with a great sense of self and purpose in this world. It has given me the strength and commitment to help in our communal recovery from the external disruptions of the past few centuries.

Find Out More

Cultural Survival Quarterly Magazine. Cultural Survival.
Reclaiming Youth at Risk: Our Hope for the Future. Larry K. Brendtro, Martin Brokenleg and Steve Van Bockern. National Educational Service. 2001.

Sidebar – Culture vs Pop Culture

Everyone who came to North America comes from a place that had a distinct culture with specific beliefs, norms, and practices. North America is full of people who have been displaced from their homelands and cultures and many do not have a connection to either of those. A lack of culture is often replaced with something that leads to the same sense of purpose and belonging. In mainstream culture this often comes in the forms of sports fanaticism, gang involvement, or heavy involvement in things such as punk rock, hip hop, or a Star Trek convention. People don't usually call it culture, but it often fills in for a lack of cultural belonging. Regalia is replaced by hockey jerseys, leather jackets, or baggy clothing and traditional dance is replaced by the Macarena or line dancing. Now, if you can see the similarities between true culture and mainstream culture you will likely have a greater appreciation for why First Nations people are so adamant about relearning, retaining, and passing on our cultural teachings to future generations.

Parenting

Traditional First Nations communities were centered on children and families. Children were considered sacred and were mentored throughout life about the traditional teachings and ways of their Nation so that they would grow to know their responsibilities and rights within their family and community. Parenting was not confined to the biological parents; rather, it was shared with grand-parents, siblings, aunts, and uncles. Other individuals also became involved in mentoring children related to the child's skills, responsibilities, and gifts. Such areas could include hunting, fishing, conducting ceremonies, gathering medicine, singing, dancing, art, and as Chiefs or Matriarchs. This nurturing environment came to a screeching halt with the introduction of residential schools. The destruction of our traditional parenting skills began when the first generation of First Nations children was forced to enter these schools. It is widely reported and accepted that residential schools were not nurturing environments; most children were not given positive attention from the adults who worked at the schools and children were often unable to see their parents for lengthy periods of time (sometimes only in the summer months, if at all). Physical punishment, ridicule, fear, and mental abuse were a regular part of daily living in the schools. Truth and Reconciliation Commission of Canada's Chair Murray Sinclair noted in his 2010 speech to the United Nations that "loneliness and fear were the Indigenous students' constant companions." Children were left to their own devices to cope with their losses, fears, and abuses that they suffered as young as five years old.

> *"Much of the instability of Indigenous families today can be directly attributed to the past practices of separating Indigenous children from their families."*
>
> Mick Dodson. 2009

The most devastating loss for First Nations people was the loss of parenting skills and healthy role models for our children to rely on for care and guidance. The forced separation of our children from their caregivers over many consecutive generations (up to eight for some communities), coupled with the negative behaviors of punishment, shame, physical and sexual abuse, and ridicule that were experienced and learned in residential schools led to the current ongoing devastation of families that has been passed on from one generation to the next, and will continue for generations to come.

The first generation of children returned home to devastated parents who faced anger, silence, and confusion in their children. Those parents would have done what they could to help their children, but likely did not learn of the abuses due to the shame and confusion the children were experiencing. Then the parents were forced to send their children back to that destructive environment after the summer break. Some children, including many Inuit children, were not sent home during the summer months due to the high cost of travel. The first generation of children to attend residential school would have had at least four years of a normal healthy childhood with their family and access to traditional healing and spiritual ceremonies that could help them recover from any abuses they suffered. These two things made the first generation of captives more likely than future generations to recover from the abuses that they had suffered and the trauma of being separated from their family, community, and culture. However, most never recovered from the experience; rather, they grew up to have children of their own and passed on some of the negative behaviors to them.

Every generation after the first would have been raised by parents who experienced the horrors of residential school, had very little, if any, access to traditional cultural teachings that would have helped them recover, and many were using alcohol to mask the pain and shame of their experiences in residential schools and for not being able to protect their own children from the schools. The cycle was solidly entrenched by the time the second or third generation of our children were stolen from us and forced into residential schools. This would continue to happen generation after generation for over 130 years to an entire people. This has left our communities without a realistic chance of a full recovery as the multi-generational experiences had normalized what is abnormal behaviour.

Today, the loss of parenting skills coupled with learned abusive behaviors results in many of our children being taken into the custody of government ministries where they are again separated from their family and traditions and often face abuses in foster homes that are supposed to keep them safe. Most First Nations children are apprehended for neglect, not abuse. Many parents still live in extreme poverty, mask their pain with their addictions, or simply do not have the skills to care for or emotionally bond with their children. This fundamental problem will continue until there is a meaningful effort by the Government of Canada to provide the supports necessary to help First Nations people to recover from the residential school experience. Until that happens, our children will continue to be raised in families that struggle to learn how to raise healthy, proud, and strong children.

Find Out More

More on parenting can be found in the 'Health & Wellness' chapter of this book.

Liberating Our Children, Liberating Our Nations. The Committee. 1992.
First Nations Child and Family Caring Society of Canada
When the Prime Minister Said Sorry. Response, Responsibility, and Renewal: Canada's Truth and Reconciliation Journey. Mick Dodson. p.118. 2009.
BALANCE: Parenting Booklet for Native Youth. Urban Native Youth Association. 2011.

Suicide

Suicide rates continue to be a strong indicator of the health and well-being of First Nations communities. Health Canada reports that the First Nations suicide rate is 5 to 7 times the national average, and is even higher for Inuit people. Youth continue to be the most vulnerable population, especially young males. There is great variance between communities and age groups, so it is difficult to have a clear picture of what is happening. However, government agencies and First Nations leaders are being aided by the important work of the Aboriginal Healing Foundation, Dr. Rod McCormick, Michael Chandler and Chris Lalonde, the National Aboriginal Health Organization, and the Centre for Suicide Prevention in better understanding and responding to this critical issue. All of these experts agree that the difference in suicide rates between communities is strongly tied to their individual community's level of autonomy, cultural continuity, educational attainment, language use, and control over community services, education, and policing. Chandler and Lalonde's research shows that community factors influence individual life affirming hopes. They report that a community's level of self-governance, court action for land title, extent of local control over health, education, and policing, facilities for the preservation of culture, local control over child welfare services, and the extent to which women are in leadership roles all play a role in the extent to which suicide is an issue in any given First Nations community.

As individual communities begin to regain their autonomy, pride, culture, traditional governance practices, and access to their resources, our young people will become more hopeful that they can have a better life. However, it is also important to note that these improvements also help to reduce social and economic conditions that lead to individual and family problems that also lead to suicide attempts. Leading experts note that the reduction of poverty, high school drop out, and unemployment rates all have a positive effects on a person's mental, emotional, and physical health which is just as important in the effort to prevent suicide. So concerted efforts must also be made in these areas now – we cannot afford to wait for treaties, land claims, or self-government before we actively work on these important issues.

Find Out More

Suicide Among Aboriginal People in Canada. Aboriginal Healing Foundation. 2007.
Suicide Crisis Response in First Nations and Inuit Communities of Canada. Dr. Rod McCormick. 2007.
Acting on What We Know: Preventing Youth Suicide in First Nations. Advisory Group on Suicide Prevention. 2003.
Cultural Continuity As A Protective Factor Against Suicide in First Nations Youth. Michael Chandler and Chris Lalonde. 2008.
Assessment and Planning Tool Kit for Suicide Prevention in First Nations Communities. National Aboriginal Health Organization. 2005.
Aboriginal Youth: A Manual of Promising Suicide Prevention Strategies. J. White and N. Jodoin. Centre for Suicide Prevention. Revised 2004.

Education

In 2006, only 67% of First Nations people ages 25-64 had completed high school compared to 87% for non-First Nations people. Those who had not finished high school had low employment rates (see section 'Employment'). Those with a university education had a very high rate of 80%; however, only 8% had attained university education which is less than one-third the non-First Nations average of 25%.

For various reasons, First Nations youth are not remaining in or doing well academically or socially in mainstream schools. The low graduation rates for our children can, in great part, be attributed to the residential school experiences for many reasons: first, the abuses that have been passed on generationally has left many First Nations people without the personal strengths and social supports needed to do well in formal educational settings; second, many people's first and only experience with formal education was through residential schools which has left them with very little respect and trust for a system that they suffered within; and third, the children who attended the schools rarely attained anything above a Grade 6 level of education. In addition to this, many believe that mainstream educational staff do not care as much as they should about whether or not our children succeed. This might be attributed to racism, a lack of resources for students with perceived social or emotional issues, or staff's general lack of caring for any students other than those that they believe are there to learn and leave their problems at home.

A prominent First Nations woman in Vancouver used to use the term 'push out rate,' rather than 'drop out rate' to describe what is happening to First Nations students in the mainstream school system. Many believe that this term more accurately reflects the forces that make it very uncomfortable and/or unsafe for our children to remain in and do well in school, both academically and socially. Systemic racism, low value for our children as learners, large class sizes, a lack of First Nations inclusion in educational materials, inaccurate and demeaning information about First Nations people being presented as truth by educators, very little personal support for children facing social issues, and funding pressures all contribute to our children being pushed out of schools. All of these factors greatly increase the likelihood of a vulnerable group's chances of leaving school whether they are First Nations or not. If a system is not willing to make meaningful change to lessen these realities, they are indeed pushing our children out of the school system.

When the day comes that we are able to get our children though secondary school, they will likely consider attending a post-secondary institution. However, there is already such a small funding pool within each community or Band to support their students, that the infusion of more students will create an even greater backlog of requests for funding. There is also talk that the Government of Canada is going to try to impose yet another policy to limit access to education funding for First Nations people. A conspiracy theorist might note the timing of this policy shift comes at the same time that First Nations people are beginning to access their rights to education in greater numbers. Some might say this is only to save money; others might say it is to save money and stop First Nations people from becoming more empowered through education, especially education that might help us to better fight against illegal and immoral policies of the Government of Canada.

Those that don't have a good understanding of the historical realities of Canada will ask "why should they have their education paid for?" Those that understand our shared history know that for centuries the Government of Canada has guaranteed to provide free education to First Nations people as a small portion of their compensation for taking over our lands. There is nothing free about an education that is promised to you in exchange for something else. We have held up our end of the bargain with the hundreds of millions of acres of land across the country while the Government of Canada has always reluctantly and barely lived up to its obligations. Each Band only receives a limited amount of funding, which has been capped at a 2%

annual increase since 1996 despite the enormous growth of the First Nations community and the increased interest of First Nations students in attending post-secondary schooling. Each individual Band has hundreds, if not thousands, of members. The amount of funding that they receive is usually only enough to fund less than 10 people at a time to go to school. Those fortunate few are in post-secondary school for at least four years, so there is only room for new applicants every four years or so. If you do the math, there is a very, very low number of people who are able to benefit from this guaranteed provision of education. The standard government line is that if First Nations Bands want to provide more funding for their students, they need to take it out of other community funding that is needed to try to effectively support their communities. It does not matter that this would literally take food out of other people's mouths. It also puts the onus on First Nations communities to subsidize the Federal government which has a responsibility to support the education of First Nations people. Until First Nations people have meaningful opportunities to attend and do well in school, both socially and academically, our communities will continue to suffer high rates of unemployment, health problems, poverty, and many other social issues.

Find Out More

Fact Sheet on First Nations Post-Secondary Education. Assembly of First Nations. 2006.
First Nations Education Steering Committee. Vancouver, B.C.
U.S. Bureau of Indian Education.
The Potential Contribution of Aboriginal Canadians to Labour Force, Employment, Productivity and Output Growth in Canada, 2001-2017. Centre for the Study of Living Standards. 2007.
Strengthening Aboriginal Success: Summary Report. Council of Ministers of Education, Canada. 2009.

Youth – A Clear Majority

The First Nations population is made up of almost 60% of people under the age of 25 and this age group is growing at three times the national average, so the percentage will continue to grow. Simply put, First Nations youth are Canada's largest untapped natural resource. Everyone is now acknowledging this, but rather than provide meaningful opportunities for First Nations youth to help fill the gap left by the retiring baby boomers, our governments are allowing companies to pay the cost of people travelling from other countries to train and be hired here. How's that for bad policy? Not to mention, shooting one's self in the foot. As long as governments continue to ignore the real needs of the First Nations community, what people view as the 'Indian Problem' will continue to exist, as without meaningful opportunities for education, training, and employment, many First Nations people will continue to rely on the social safety net to survive. Why not take the time to educate and train First Nations youth, either formally or informally through on the job training? Statistics continue to show that when First Nations people graduate high school, they often go on to post-secondary education and those that have at least a bachelor's degree are highly employable. I know, I know, it takes a long time to educate and train people. But, how long have governments known that there would be a large need now? I've been hearing about it every five years when Statistics Canada releases census reports that show the population growth, un/employment numbers, educational attainment, and many other statistics that add to the clear-cut case that First Nations youth need to have meaningful opportunities in order for them to reach their full potential.

Will this be like treaties – wait until they are settled before really tackling issues that will help to strengthen the First Nations community, and therefore Canada? Delaying action is only delaying dealing with the issue; it is not solving the problem that affects both First Nations and non-First Nations people. I know there will be those who say "First Nations people just need to get a job' or 'pull up their socks' or some other equally un-helpful response. If those people read from the beginning of this book, they will begin to truly understand how outside forces have left many First Nations people and communities struggling. Then they will know that simply providing jobs, good ones or not, is not the answer needed to make real and sustainable change.

When I see many First Nations organizations, political organizations, or Chiefs and Council, I often see a brown reflection of mainstream society – mostly middle-aged men in leadership positions. There are some youth advisory councils in First Nations political organizations, but often youth are confronted with a rude awakening when they come to the realization that they are often only tokenized. They are not even given a youth seat on the main committee, just a sub-committee with no real influence. Most often youth are not paid to be there and sometimes have to skip school to make daytime meetings, but they attend anyways as they are enthusiastic about contributing to positive change for their peers and community. However, many youth become frustrated and leave as their voices are sometimes stifled and/or ignored. For many First Nations youth, their growing frustration comes from both outside and within the First Nations community. Their frustrations are usually valid. Even if youth sometimes ask for what may seem to be 'too much' or unrealistic, explain why you can't meet that request, rather than patronizingly agreeing with them or disregarding them. Until we truly empower First Nations youth to contribute to their community and the Canadian economy, they will continue to transition into adulthood with few skills and resources to live independently successfully. It would do us all well to remember that we will rely on these young people to look after us and our interests someday.

<u>Find Out More</u>

The Potential Contribution of Aboriginal Canadians to Labour Force, Employment, Productivity and Output Growth in Canada, 2001-2017. Centre for the Study of Living Standards.

2007.
Urban Aboriginal Youth: An Action Plan for Change. Standing Senate Committee on Aboriginal Peoples. 2003.
Guidelines for the Engagement of Young People. First Nations Child & Family Caring Society of Canada.
An Exploration of Aboriginal Youth Engagement. Cheryl Matthew. Centre for Native Policy and Research.
Urban Aboriginal Peoples Study Report. Environics Institute. 2010.
Hope or Heartbreak: Aboriginal Youth and Canada's Future from Horizons: Policy Research Initiative. Government of Canada. 2008.
Redwire Magazine
Say Magazine
New Tribe Magazine

Sexuality

A healthy sense of sexuality amongst First Nations people is rare, as it is in mainstream society. There is still so much to talk about and do before we can ensure that our people are learning to have a healthy sense of sexuality again. In 2008, Drew Hayden Taylor nudged the discussion along with *Me Sexy* in which he highlights the many ways that First Nations people are expressing their sexuality – he says that First Nations' sexuality is often overlooked by mainstream society which may be led to believe that First Nations people are not enjoying sex or that they do have a healthy sense of sexuality due to the media's focus on sexual abuse, sexual exploitation, and HIV/AIDS in our community. Others such as Martin Cannon look into the distant past to pinpoint when First Nations' views of sexuality changed and why. He brings to light the colonial efforts to christianize First Nations people, which included the regulation of our sexuality as only being heterosexual and to be hidden. Norval Morriseau celebrated human sexuality through many of his erotic paintings, which are some of the least known of his work; and Daphne Odjig, who was fortunate to grow up in a time and place when sexuality was not associated with shame, had little hesitation in providing the erotic art for *Tales from the Smokehouse* in 1974. These are a few of the artists who were pushing the boundaries that were imposed upon First Nations people to try to help us shed the cloak of shame that others have taught us.

The National Aboriginal Health Organization's First Nations Centre notes that to have good sexual health First Nations people must have access to information related to many aspects of sexuality including sex, gender identities and roles, sexual orientation, eroticism, pleasure, intimacy and reproduction. Without these important things, a person's sense of sexuality and sex can become skewed. There are many areas of concern for First Nations people that stem from an unhealthy sense of sexuality whether it came about because an individual was taught to not talk about or express their sexuality, or by being sexually exploited or abused. Some of the fallout can include early pregnancy, sexual exploitation, sexual abuse, sexually transmitted disease, and homophobia. There are a few important initiatives and organizations have been working to combat some of the issues that inhibit a healthy sense of sexuality amongst First Nations people. The Native Youth Sexual Health Network (NYSHN) provides leadership in starting open communication on various issues related to a person's sexuality in order to promote healthy self-esteem and sexuality among First Nations youth. NYSHN also produces reports, videos, and other learning materials as resources to help others learn about and promote healthy sexuality. 2-Spirited People of the First Nations has worked for many years to remind people of the proud traditional teachings regarding Two-spirit, lesbian, gay, and transgender people, support research in this area, and provide a safe place for community members to be themselves.

One area that is still difficult for people to talk about or confront is sexual abuse of children. It is clear that First Nations people's sense of sexuality has become skewed due to the sexual abuse that occurred at most residential schools generation after generation. It can be easy to learn unhealthy behaviors if they are taught to you long enough, but it is much harder to unlearn them. Some of those children who were sexually abused in residential schools grew up to abuse children themselves, then some of those victims grew up to abuse the next generation of children, and so on, and so on. When you couple this learned sexual deviance with a loss of healing ceremonies, healthy communication, emotional attachments, and family structure you can understand how this has become a problem. There are those in the First Nations community who will be furious that I am suggesting that this is a problem in First Nations communities, but that is not my main concern. Rather, it is a distraction from the real issues, and I won't be a part of that. According to my ancestors, I have a responsibility for the seven generations to come – I am not responsible for ensuring that silence and shame continue to erode our communities. There are others who will be glad that I am writing this as they understand that meaningful change cannot come about until we acknowledge there is a problem and do something about it. Unless someone is a part of the solution, they are a part of the problem: as in this instance doing nothing is allowing it to continue. Silence and shame are leading victims of sexual abuse to end their own lives either slowly through unhealthy behaviors and coping mechanisms or immediately by suicide. We have the power to end the cycle of sexual abuse within our own families, communities, and beyond. So, we have to be brave enough to each do our part in ensuring that it at least stops in our own homes, families, and communities. Our children deserve to have healthy and safe childhoods that many of us never had.

<u>Find Out More</u>

Me Sexy: An Exploration of Native Sex and Sexuality. Drew Haydon Taylor. Douglas & McIntyre. 2008.

Native Youth Sexual Health Network

Norval Morrisseau: Return to the House of Invention. Joseph and Norval Morrisseau. 2006.

Odjig: The Art of Daphne Odjig 1966-2000: The Art of Daphne Odjig, 1966-2000. B. Boyer and C. Podedworny. 2002.

The Regulation of First Nations Sexuality. M. Cannon. The Canadian Journal of Native Studies, Vol. XVIII, Issue 1, p. 1-18. 2010.

Aboriginal Sexual Offending in Canada. Dr. J.H. Hylton, M. Bird, N. Eddy, H. Sinclair, and H. Stenerson. Aboriginal Healing Foundation. 2002.

National Aboriginal Health Organization's First Nations Centre

2-Spirit People of the First Nations Society

Communications

Communication tools are essential to help disseminate and receive information. For First Nations communities, geography plays a large role in the amount and type of communications tools that are accessible. Although it seems that everyone in North America would have access to all of today's modern conveniences, that is not always the case. For instance, some First Nations communities in the North or in remote areas may not have access to television or internet, but may be able to pick up some radio stations. For these communities, radio becomes very important in relaying and receiving information. There are a growing number of First Nations people providing the resources for First Nations people and communities to stay informed and in touch despite their level of access to modern communication tools. They are building a communication highway through newspapers, radio, websites, television, and email.

First Nations newspapers are read primarily by First Nations people, but many more can benefit by reading the unique stories, commentary, and even jokes. You can usually find free copies in First Nations organizations or sometimes in small bookstores: so what have you got to lose by checking them out? These papers focus primarily on First Nations issues in a particular region or community, but their stories are universal. These papers can be great marketing tools for businesses or government bodies that don't have direct access to a particular community, and it has the added benefit of helping to support the production and distribution of these community-based newspapers. There are very few national newspapers other than Indian Country Today and the Native American Times in the United States, but there are a fair number of small regional newspapers. Some of the larger ones include Nunavut's Kivalliq News, Ontario's Anishinabek News, and western Canada's Aboriginal Multi-Media Society which publishes a number of the major First Nations newspapers and utilizes their website to disseminate information. Nation Talk is a new online news source dedicated to First Nations issues.

The Aboriginal Peoples Television Network came into being in 1997 to great applause from First Nations people and others interested in finding out more about Canada's First People. For over a decade, APTN has grown to include entertainment shows, drama series, comedies, festivals, investigative reports, documentaries, and a daily national newscast with First Nations reporters and from a First Nations' perspective. I can't wait to see what they do next. Some smaller and remote communities are utilizing community television stations to host shows or use free community information channels to post notices. Radio stations such as Aboriginal Voices Radio are beginning to pop up across the country in larger urban markets. First Nations individuals are also utilizing small rural and urban radio stations to host their own First Nations-focused shows which highlight First Nations artists and issues. Others are utilizing the internet to write, produce, and host their own shows.

Young people are especially active in using social media and are beginning to make huge contributions in this area through their music, commentary, and volunteerism. Websites and social media such as Facebook and MySpace are quickly becoming quite popular in First Nations communities that have access to the internet. Since there is no central body to receive and disseminate information, it is important for communities to be able to get their message out, and the internet is a good way to reach a broad audience. Unfortunately, despite the Government of Canada's valiant attempt a few years back to bring internet access to most remote communities, many First Nations communities still do not have access. In 2009, over one-third of B.C. First Nations communities still did not have broadband access. In addition, although there may be internet access in a community, the high level of poverty amongst First Nations people does not allow for many to own computers and routers or to pay for internet services, so they cannot enjoy the same level of access as others do. For some First Nations communities, especially in the United States, even phone access is limited. If they also do not have internet access, then they can't even take advantage of the growing trend to make long distance calls over the internet. The lack of access to internet, phone, and text services is sometimes due simply to the sheer size of the territory, and a lack of infrastructure funds to expand upon the mainstream communications highway to ensure everyone has equal access. So despite vast technological advances and our world shrinking as globalization forges ahead via the internet, First Nations people are still decades behind due to remoteness and poverty. If we can put massive satellites in space so that we can talk to people as they visit the moon, then surely we can ensure that everyone has fair and equitable access to the basic communications infrastructure that most people in North America have.

Although there are definite benefits to having access to technology that allows people to reach outside of their community, there are also some very real concerns. In some cases, access to the internet is making vulnerable individuals even more vulnerable to being exploited. Young women are being lured out of their rural communities by those who are looking for someone to exploit. Once they are convinced that they are in love with the person wooing them over the internet or that they can get a job in the city, they are often sent a one-way ticket to large urban areas where they are eventually forced into the drug or sex trade. Safety issues surrounding the internet, text messaging, and other communication tools are only now starting to enter people's minds. Groups such as Safe On-Line Outreach Society (SOLOS) and Childnet International are working tirelessly online and in schools, organizations, and board rooms to help raise awareness about these issues.

Find Out More

Aboriginal People's Television Network
AMS List of Canada's Aboriginal Publications
Turtle Island Web
Aboriginal Voices Radio Station (Vancouver, Calgary,

Edmonton, Toronto, Ottawa)
Indian Country Today Newspaper (U.S., national)
First Nations Technology Council
Pathways to Technology Project
Redwire Magazine
Say Magazine
New Tribe Magazine
Revision Quest. Darrell Dennis. CBC Radio.
NationTalk Online News
Safe On-Line Outreach Society (SOLOS)
Childnet International

DISCONNECTED YOUTH

Chapter 4

Fairness & Justice

First Nations

Indigenous

INUIT

Aboriginal

First People

Off-Reserve

STATUS

METIS

On-Reserve

Non-Status

Native

What's in a Name?

I am one of those people who believes that language and words are important. Words, when used improperly or maliciously, can hurt, diminish, or belittle the importance of something. I insist that First Nations, Native, Aboriginal, and Tsimshian all be capitalized as they describe an entire people, just like Italian and Japanese do. Elder and Chief are equally important as they hold very important and distinguished places within First Nations communities, just like Mayors, Chiefs of Police, or Premiers do in mainstream communities.

While some First Nations people embrace the term 'Indian,' many do not. Many of those who do use it, especially in the United States, do so as they are referred to as 'Indians' in treaties and other government documents, which are the basis for their legal and political relationship with federal and state governments. Some will only use it amongst other First Nations people. Most who do not use it, do not because we do not believe that we should embrace a term that was forced upon us by an explorer who got lost on his way to India to find spices. In the USA, the terms most widely accepted are Native American, American Indian, and Alaskan Native. In Canada, the term First Nations is more widely accepted as it was chosen in consultation with First Nations people, and it acknowledges that we were here first and that we are made up of many distinct Nations. Unfortunately, over the last few years, many politicians and on-reserve people have started to use the name 'First Nations' only to refer to on-reserve people as a way of distinguishing themselves for governments who need to have these sorts of things spelled out for them I guess. Once again, our actions and names are being dictated by an outside source rather than us defining what we are called as a people. It is not up to politicians, First Nations or not, to tell me or any other First Nations person who we are and what we should be called.

The current 'all inclusive' term used in Canada is 'Aboriginal'. I personally do not like the word, as most words starting with 'ab' mean 'not'. As in 'not original'. I have recently started using the term ANoriginal, as that is what each of us is: an original or Indigenous person of this land now called Canada. 'Indigenous' used to be used mainly by grassroots people, but many others are now realizing the strength in using this term as it better reflects our reality. As with many other Indigenous people around the world, we are Indigenous to our lands, therefore we are Indigenous People. As Indigenous People, we usually seek out other Indigenous People when we travel, and we instantly know that these people have had similar atrocities forced upon them by colonizing nations, but we also know that they have core cultural beliefs that will be similar to our own.

I used to wonder what my traditional last name would have been. Then one day I realized that we did not have last names like we do now, so I have not lost anything in that sense. All across Canada, there are very few First Nations people who hold their ancestral names. While we did not have names in the forms that they are now, first/middle/last, we did have names that could have been adapted to the new system. However, the colonizers had no interest in helping us keep any connection to our traditional ways or names. While some names have survived, many have not. Many in the east have French names or those of men who came to their territories. In B.C., many of our last names are those of the Indian agents who were around during those times. Apparently, they were not very creative - but were more than a little vain. Once they ran out of men's first names like Charlie, James, Willie, Johnny, Bob, Wilson, or Jim, they moved on to colors. Not very creative or caring I would say. I as a 'Gray', have an aunt who was a 'Green' and friends who are 'Whites' and 'Browns'. How's that for a history to bear.

Constitutional Rights

First Nations people from across Canada fought for decades to ensure that our issues and concerns stayed at the forefront of politics in Canada. All of their efforts, from small to enormous, led to our inherent rights being enshrined into the Canadian *Constitution* when it was repatriated from England in 1982. The most well-known grassroots action that took place was the Constitution Express which saw hundreds of First Nations people board a train at various points across the country on a pilgrimage of sorts to Ottawa to ensure that our rights as First Nations people were enshrined in the new *Constitution.* This action, amongst many others, led to the inclusion of Section 35 of the *Constitution* which states that "the existing aboriginal and treaty rights of the aboriginal people of Canada are hereby affirmed." Having this enshrined in the *Constitution* put a formal stop to the arbitrary extinguishment of some First Nations' rights, and it is the best we could get at the time. However, it is extremely far from what it should be since we still have to fight to retain the few rights that we have and we have to fight even harder to have them adhered to by the Government of Canada.

While those of us who know the significance of having Section 35 in the *Constitution,* are thrilled that it is there, we are also painfully aware that this vague wording has left plenty of opportunity for successive Canadian governments to abdicate their fiduciary responsibility to First Nations people. Any and all claims to inherent rights to land and resources must relate back to our constitutional rights as First Nations people before they are taken seriously by the courts. The wording does not make it easy for First Nations people to assert their rights. Rather, we are forced to prove that the asserted rights were common practice before the first immigrants came to *our* shores, even though our cultures always evolved over time to meet with current reality. Significant cases decided by the Supreme Court of Canada include land rights in *Delgamuukw v. British Columbia* (1997), fishing rights in *Sparrow v. the Queen* (1990), and Métis hunting rights in *R. v. Powley* (2003). Each of these cases was determined on how well the First Nations person or Nation was able to trace back their history even though the ability to do so has been irrevocably damaged by previous government action which vigorously attempted to eliminate First Nations culture, values, history, language, and connection to traditional territories. This task is made almost impossible when courts insist that our oral history does not count as reliable testimony.

One of the most difficult areas to get the Government of Canada, the provinces, and territories to adhere to is the duty to consult with First Nations people regarding actions that may affect our interests. The duty to consult is required even if the affected First Nations has not yet proven a claim to the land. The prime example is in the use of reserve land and traditional territories. Many First Nations are forced to spend millions of dollars to launch court cases in order to ensure that governments are fulfilling their legal duty to consult with First Nations peoples and accommodate our interests when considering actions that will affect us. The duty to consult is grounded in the principle of the honour of the Crown when dealing with First Nations people and has been affirmed in *Haida Nation v. British Columbia* (2004), *Taku River Tlingit First Nation v. British Columbia* (2004), and *Mikisew Cree First Nation v. Canada* (2005).

While it is not the belief of most First Nations people that we should have to prove our right to our land and resources, we are forced to work within a foreign system which has been imposed upon us despite the existence of treaties or unceded territories. Until such a day comes when we no longer have to adhere to the Canadian justice system at the expense of our own, we will have to play by their rules in order to have access to what is rightfully and inherently ours.

Find Out More

The Crown's Constitutional Duty to Consult and Accommodate Aboriginal and Treaty Rights. The National Centre for First Nations Governance. 2008.

Canada's Indigenous Constitution. John Borrows. University of Toronto Press. 2010.

The U.S. Constitution and the Great Law of Peace: A Comparison of Two Founding Documents. J. Swamp and G. Schaaf. Center for Indigenous Arts & Culture. 2004.

Terms of Reference for a Mi'kmaq-Nova Scotia - Canada Consultation Process. 2010.

Treaties

Historic and modern-day treaties between First Nations and 'new governments' have been around for well over 100 years. Many people believe that treaties and land claims are the same thing, but they are not. While both are 'claims' to land, a treaty is developed out of a comprehensive land claim that asserts an Aboriginal right and title that have not been dealt with by treaty or other legal means. Specific land claims are pursued to address non-fulfillment of a treaty or improper administration of lands and other assets of treaties or other legal obligations. The establishment of historical treaties enabled the government to expand and continue with immigrant settlement, land distribution, agriculture, and other economic activities. The most well-know treaties are the eleven Numbered Treaties which were signed between 1871 and 1921 and covered Northern Ontario, Manitoba, Saskatchewan, Alberta, and parts of the Yukon, the Northwest Territories and a tiny portion of British Columbia. Other activities include the Peace and Friendship Treaties (1725-1779), Upper Canada Land Surrenders (1764-1862), Robinson Treaties (1850), Douglas Treaties (1850-54), and Williams Treaties (1923). The most significant (in terms of size) modern day activity dealt with a large part of Canada's north involving the Inuit with four treaties and agreements signed between 1975-2005 covering various areas from the Northwest Territories to Labrador. The first modern day treaty in British Columbia was signed in 1999, with only a few more following since then.

While the signing of treaties provided certainty for the government, it was not so for First Nations people as often treaties were not fulfilled which has resulted in large numbers of land claims being filed over the years. In many cases, First Nations were not given the land that was promised in the treaties, or the land was taken away at a later date without permission or compensation. In 2008, the National Centre for First Nations Governance (NCFNG) produced a research report which provided an historic overview of the major legal cases that were launched by First Nations in response to successive governments infringing upon their rights or not fulfilling their fiduciary duty in implementing treaties. The NCFNG states that research makes it clear that the "current law confirms that the Crown must act in the best interest of the Indian people, where required. The Crown will always know the content of historical treaties and cannot claim that it was unaware of the nature of its obligations toward Treaty First Nations." Since 1973, there have been 1,308 specific claims submitted to Canada. As of 2009, only 543 of these claims had been concluded and 765 remained outstanding. There were 131 specific claims in negotiations across the country and 34 claims with the Indian Specific Claims Commission. Many years of pressure by the Assembly of First Nations (AFN) forced the federal government to create the Specific Claims Tribunal in 2008 to decrease the backlog of claims. The Tribunal makes binding decisions on outstanding claims that have not been acknowledged by the government within three years of being submitted, were rejected by the government, or where an agreement was not reached after three years. According to the AFN, at the end of 2005 there were over one thousand unsettled land claims and, up to that time, there were on average only eight claims settled each year. At that rate, it would take 130 years to resolve all claims.

B.C. Modern Day Treaties

In British Columbia, less than 5% of First Nation's land was ever ceded (surrendered) through treaties or other legal means. Up until 1999, when the Nisga'a Nation signed the first modern day treaty in B.C., only a very small portion of Vancouver Island known as the Douglas Treaties and the small northeast corner of B.C. that was a part of Treaty 8 were a part of a treaty. While there are First Nations who do not want to sign treaties, there are others who have been struggling for decades under the government's system, timelines, and rules, to try to bring some finality and certainty for their people. A prime example of this is the length of time it took for the Nisga'a Nation to force the federal government to negotiate their treaty which they had been striving for since 1890. For decades they were ignored, then faced new laws which made it illegal to raise funds for land claims challenges. In the 1960s the Nisga'a began legal action in the B.C. Supreme Court, but it wasn't until 1976 that the federal government entered treaty negotiations with the Nisga'a, and the B.C. government did not join the negotiations until 1990. The Nisga'a Nation's epic journey is just one example of the long and ongoing struggle by First Nations in B.C. to come to terms with the governments of B.C. and Canada regarding their traditional unceded territories.

The Auditor General of British Columbia's 2006 report showed that the B.C. government spent approximately $260 million from 1993 to 2005 on the B.C. Treaty Process. The Auditor General of Canada reported in 2006 that the B.C. treaty negotiations were badly bogged down, that the Government of Canada had spent $426 million from 1993-2006, and that B.C. First Nations had borrowed close to $300 million. Both reports note that the treaty process was flawed, but that the settlement of treaties would help bring economic certainty for B.C. and Canada, as well as for First Nations in B.C. By 2003, almost 80 interim measurement agreements were signed, but not one treaty was successfully negotiated through the B.C. treaty process. The lone treaty which was negotiated with the Nisga'a was accomplished outside of the formal treaty process. The federal report likely contributed to the recent progress in B.C. with four treaties, being ratified by each First Nation's membership: Tsawwassen (2009), Lheidli T'enneh (2011), Yale (2011), and Maa-nulth (2011). The BC Treaty Commission highlights the 2009 Price Waterhouse report which validated previous reports that estimated that the resolution of treaties in B.C. could add $10 billion dollars to B.C's economy over the following 15 years. Among other things, B.C.'s six-stage treaty process can result in treaties that address many things including land, food harvesting, self-governance, culture, natural resources, duty of governments to consult First Nations, and financial compensation for lost land and resources.

The logistics of negotiating a new treaty or a land claim can be very frustrating for First Nations people as they are pursued in both a foreign system that was imposed upon First Nations people and we are forced to pay vast amounts of money fighting for our inherent rights which are enshrined in the Canadian *Constitution*. The case of First Nations in British Columbia highlights this financial burden which resulted in First Nations borrowing over $300 million dollars to pursue treaties between 1993 – 2005 with not a single treaty being signed during that time period through the B.C. treaty process. This is just a drop in the bucket of what has and will be spent by First Nations in pursuing their inherent rights through treaties and land claims in Canada. The other major hurdle for First Nations is that the governmental and court systems do not view our oral histories as valid 'proof' of our claims to land and other resources. This imposed view of what is valid and what is not, especially in B.C. where almost the entire province is still not secured by the government, puts First Nations people at a disadvantage as they struggle to meet standards of proof within an foreign imposed system.

Find Out More

What's the deal with treaties? A layperson's guide to treaty making in British Columbia. B.C. Treaty Commission.
UBCIC: Stolen Lands Broken Promises.
Treaty Relationships Between the Canadian and American Governments and First Nation Peoples. National Centre for First Nations Governance. 2008.
Financial and Economic Impacts of Treaty Settlements in British Columbia. Price Waterhouse. 2009.
Treaty Negotiations in British Columbia: An Assessment of the Effectiveness of British Columbia's Management and Administrative Processes. Office of the Auditor General of British Columbia. 2006.

Oral Traditions in the Courtroom

> *"We are an oral people: history, law, politics, sociology, the self, and our relationship to the world are all contained in our memory. Home is for us origin, the shell of nurturance, our first fire and the harbinger of our relationship to the world."*
>
> Lee Maracle. My Home As I Remember. 2000

The foundation of First Nations culture is our oral traditions. In addition to such things as pictographs, dances, and songs, the main way of recording and preserving our history was through passing on the stories and history of our people verbally. First Nations people deeply value our oral traditions, but we cannot say the same for governments and courts in Canada or the United States. While our Elders and history keepers are able to meaningfully and articulately recount our histories in their traditional territories, their recollections are usually not believed or accepted as 'proof' of what we claim is true. If it were written down on a leaf from 400 years ago, we might have a better chance of having our recounting believed. A prime example of this is when Justice McEachern of the B.C. Supreme Court of Canada in *Delgamu'ukw v. Canada* completely discounted the importance and validity of our oral teachings by refusing to believe the testimony of our Elders.

When thinking about this issue, one must remember that this is all based on a foreign justice system that has been imposed on First Nations people. While we did not have any influence on the development of the overall justice system, we are profoundly and negatively impacted by it on a daily basis. This is especially true for those First Nations who have not signed treaties or ceded their traditional territories. In order for First Nations to regain our traditional territories, we must argue our case in a foreign and imposed court system which we have never bought into. Imagine if I came into your house and took over. I've allowed you to live in the tattered garage without access to the resources available in the main house such as water, hydro, or a stove to cook on. When you complain, I let you know that there is now a new system of authority because you supposedly did not put up a good enough fight against my actions. So I inform you that you can try to rectify my alleged wrong doings against you by submitting a claim to my court which is severely backlogged, in another city, and it will cost you more than you could ever afford so I will lend you the money to fight against my system, and I will only accept evidence on my terms which includes only those things recorded on 100% recycled rain forest paper which has been written on by a platinum pen and witnessed by particular people. This sounds ridiculous, but it is essentially what is happening to First Nations people across North America. The argument is made that it is now a different time with different rules and systems to address such things, but those rules and systems weren't in place when First Nations people signed treaties. However, other ones were that must be abided by no matter how long ago they were in effect. If we are to go by today's laws, then we must recognize that contracts and treaties that are signed today will be enforced 80 years from now based on the laws and policies that were in place at the time of the signing. This is common practice and knowledge for governments and business, so ignorance is not an option, nor is changing the rules and agreements only when it comes to dealing with First Nations people.

Fishing, Hunting, and Gathering

In the past few decades the issue of First Nations peoples' right to fish, hunt, and gather has become quite controversial and has often gone before the courts. This is primarily due to fish and lobster stocks declining which left non-First Nations fishers' livelihoods in jeopardy. Up until that time, there was little worry about First Nations doing what they had done since time immemorial, as long as others could become rich from the industries that they created. Once that was jeopardized, due to over-fishing and poor management by the Canadian and United States governments, First Nations people's inherent rights were challenged. And in fact, First Nations people were blamed for the declining stocks due to over-fishing despite there being no evidence to support such an outlandish claim given that most of our people still fish on the river with nets.

Those who have not taken the time to try to find out the truth are convinced that First Nations people are stockpiling fish up and down the Fraser River in British Columbia. Have these people seen the small nets that are used and the often challenging locations we fish in? Likely not, as they are not interested in the truth. Rather, they want someone to blame. Do First Nations people sometimes sell the fish that they catch? Yes. We have an inherent and constitutional right to fish, hunt, and gather. First Nations people have always bartered and traded in order to get the things that we do not have readily available to us. Just look at the grease trails that First Nations people used to travel to other communities to trade oolichan grease for food or goods. We traded animal pelts with non-First Nations people for food and other necessities. Since we are no longer in the pre-1900s, we do not have to travel great distances to trade for meat, shells, or tools, but we still have the right to trade for what we need. Today, we are able to convert the fish to money, which we use to buy or 'trade' for the goods that we need such as electricity, diapers, or food. This is the exact same thing, just a different context in which we are forced to live due the colonization of North America. In fact, I often have to go trade money for canned salmon at the local grocer since I do not have access to my traditional territories and therefore cannot practice my right to fish.

In recent years, both First Nations and Métis people have been successful in asserting their inherent rights to hunt and gather food. As many know, First Nations people have always been hunters and gatherers; this has not changed since contact and I assume it never will. We hunt animals of all sizes, as well as gather berries and medicinal plants. The main difference between First Nations people and non-First Nations people is that we view this whole process as spiritual in nature. We acknowledge the animal or plant spirit that has given its life in order that we might eat and survive. This is not to say that all First Nations people still practice these important traditions, but there are many who do. Also trophy hunting is not something that is usually found amongst First Nations people as it is in the non-First Nations community where animals are killed for sport and the carcasses left to rot or are sold to a hide manufacturer. First Nations people hunt for food and use the hide to make drums, regalia, jackets, or moccasins; we don't pay a taxidermist to mount it for us so it can be displayed on our walls. People will do what they will do, but I find it ridiculous and insulting that our right to hunt for food is less important than trophy hunting because it is now an industry to make money from.

Despite the continuity of traditional hunting practices and court cases won, there is still very little access to wild game and fish for the average First Nations person. Reasons include a lack of hunting and fishing knowledge and gear, that many areas have been deforested so the animals have relocated, and that many rivers have been polluted or destroyed due to logging, mining and other industries, and being restricted by having to obtain a licence which can be hard when you have no money or transportation to get to far away offices.

Find Out More

The Cohen Commission of Inquiry into the Decline of the Sockey Salmon in the Fraser River.

Regina v. Powley: A Summary of the Supreme Court of Canada Reason for Judgment. Pape & Salter. Métis harvesting rights. 2003.

Spotlight – Constitutional Right to Harvest

In Canadian law, members of a First Nation have the right under Section 35 of the *1982 Constitution Act* to trade and barter in fish or wildlife harvested by them if their ancestors traded or bartered in these items at the time of contact with Europeans, and trade and barter was an important part of the culture of the First Nation. The Tsawwassen (2009) and Maa-nulth (2011) treaties simplify and strengthen this right to trade and barter. Both treaties contain provisions recognizing the right of members of these First Nations to trade and barter in fish and aquatic plants, wildlife and migratory birds among themselves and with other Aboriginal people who are resident in B.C. This right is subject to any laws made by the First Nations. For these two Nations, trade and barter does not include sale. However, the sale of fish or wildlife by members is permitted if it is authorized by federal law (for fish and migratory birds) and provincial law for other wildlife.

Racism

It is really quite sad and maddening that in this day and age, anyone has to contend with racism in North America. Both Canada and the U.S. assert that they are a cultural mosaic and melting pot respectively. Of these two, Canada has the better motto. Canada supposedly encourages cultural difference and acceptance, while the U.S. encourages assimilation and sameness. Although Canada is becoming quite diverse, there is no true effort by the Canadian Government to ensure that current residents or new immigrants have any understanding of what living in a culturally diverse country means, especially in relations to First Nations people. This neglect encourages ignorance which breeds racism and discrimination. Most people do not understand our history, circumstances, unique place within Canada, or the true facts on hot button topics such as fishing, treaties, housing, and education. It is most often left up to First Nations people themselves to counteract the racist beliefs and actions, rather than people in positions of influence and power stepping up and helping to eradicate this racism which affects all people, not just First Nations people. Many First Nations people are willing and able to conduct anti-racism, cultural competency, cross cultural, cultural awareness, and other similar workshops for businesses, individuals, sports teams, and governments alike, but the overall lack of interest and commitment leaves them working in other jobs so that they can feed their families.

First Nations people continue to endure high rates of racist acts and physical attacks against us. One cannot ignore this issue when our youth are continually being pushed out of the mainstream school system or being harassed by police, our women continue to go missing and be murdered, we continue to be victims of hate crimes, we are still used as mascots for sports teams, our athletes still have racial slurs hurled at them, we are represented in derogatory ways in television and film, and we continue to hear racist rants while non-First Nations fishermen and others declare that they are the victims of reverse racism. At the same time, misinformation runs rampant as people refuse to look beyond the headlines to see what the truth is. A recent example is from November 2010 when the Canadian Taxpayers Federation (CTF) published salary figures for First Nation Chiefs and Councillors without clarifying that much of the totals included expense reimbursements that were not in fact income. They distorted the information so much that they were comparing apples to bananas and the Assembly of First Nations (AFN) was forced to produce *The Straight Goods on First Nations Salaries* so that the average person could have access to the truth. Unfortunately, the AFN's report did not garner the same headlines as the CTF's did.

Find Out More

Reel Injun: On the Trail of the Hollywood Indian. Neil Diamond. Rezolution Pictures. 2009.
The Straight Goods on First Nations Salaries. Assembly of First Nations. November 2010.
Indigenous Cultural Competency Training. BC Provincial Health Services Authority.
Working Effectively With Aboriginal People. Indigenous Corporate Training Inc.

Rant – We Are Not Mascots

I cannot understand how people can claim that it is not offensive to First Nations people to be parodied as mascots while also having parts of our culture appropriated and distorted beyond recognition. I do not believe that it is necessary for the Atlanta Braves baseball team to have a First Nations man (aka a brave) wielding a tomahawk to evoke a competitive spirit, fear, or whatever else they are thinking. When seeing this mascot or uniform logo, I am sure that the overwhelming majority of people do not conjure up images of a First Nations people in a positive way, if they even think of us at all. Even if someone does not consciously think about the implications of using First Nations people as goofy mascots, psychologists will tell you that it still has a subconscious effect on how they view First Nations people. This would be especially true for children. For those who argue, and I mean vehemently argue, that it is okay to do so would likely have a fit if something near and dear to them was used in the same way. In fact, when caricatures of a Jewish man, Asian man, and Jesus were produced to illustrate how wrong it is to depict First Nations people this way, people were outraged and lives were threatened. Those pictures caused an uproar because they made people look at it from a place that negatively affected them; you could say they were forced to walk a mile in our moccasins! This action no doubt changed some people's minds about it being an honor for First Nations to be used as mascots for sports teams.

Inappropriate Phrases

There are many phrases that are bandied about without much thought and without empathy for the people that they are directly related to. In most cases, these phrases are simply used as a weapon to hurt people. In this case, it is First Nations people. While there are many terms that can be talked about here, the following are the most common ones that I hope you never use now or in the future:

- 'Indian Time' – Today's cheapest excuse for being late is to label lateness as 'Indian Time'. Using this term in common day-to-day situations dilutes its meaning and importance. The appropriate use of this term would be when time has less significance and things are more in tune with traditional cultural practices. For instance, I might use it when there is a community gathering that is going longer than anticipated because an Elder unexpectedly spoke to impart some teaching. So since this is a natural part of our existence, it would be appropriate to say it ended on Indian time. But, if I simply was late showing up because I didn't wake up on time, or stopped to get tea, that is simply poor time management. To give it cultural significance, is insulting.

- 'Low Man on the Totem Pole' – Totem poles are not based on hierarchy and power in the way that many people think they are, so using this term is inaccurate and discounts the significant meaning of a traditional totem pole. Totem poles are an artistic representation of the history of the person or group it was made for, represents a significant event, or honors a Nation's clans. A totem pole may have the head of the house on the top of the pole, but it did not mean that they were better or more important than the others.

- 'Chief' – is a common term that is sometimes used to replace the term 'boss' or 'leader', but that is very rare. It is usually used to refer to First Nations people despite any prompting from us or discussion about how we feel about the term being used in this way. While others think it is cute or funny, most of us do not. Traditionally, our Chiefs worked hard to earn that title; it was not given out willy-nilly. So to use it so casually and inappropriately, is to dilute its significance.

- The terms 'on the warpath' or 'putting on your war paint' are not used to honor our warriors of the past; rather, they are used to insinuate that we are a war faring people who need little reason to attack others.

- 'Off the reservation' – This phrase isn't used to talk about First Nations people going into town to shop or visit; rather, it usually refers to people going wild and/or against what is right or accepted.

- The Washington NFL football team may think that the term 'redskin' is in some distorted way an honor to First Nations people, but the large backlash should have been enough to make them change it as soon as they realized how grossly inappropriate it is to use. In an attempt to exterminate First Nations people, in the 1600s the United States paid a bounty to anyone who could kill and bring in a 'red skin'. This included not only men, but women and children also.

- 'Eskimo' – It's enough for us to know that most Inuit people view this term as derogatory. So stop saying it, using it on food items, or for names of sports teams.

Find Out More
What's in a Name? Greg Garber. espn.com.

Veterans

First Nations people have been helping Canada fight in wars since The War of 1812 when Canada and the British took up arms against the Americans. Veterans Affairs Canada reports that over 7,000 First Nations people, and an unknown number of Métis, Inuit, and non-status people, served in the First and Second World Wars and the Korean War. The First Nations Veterans Association estimates that 12,000 men and women served in those wars. Since then, many First Nations individuals have continued to enlist in Canada's armed forces right up until present day. The Canadian military has recently increased their efforts to recruit First Nations youth through the Bold Eagle and other similar programs. Today's recruitment strategies include using cultural traditions, images, and phrases that are culturally relevant such as 'a proud tradition' or 'warrior spirit' in order to recruit our youth into the armed forces. These strategies will help to ensure First Nations people are involved in higher numbers. Many First Nations people are opposed to the recruitment of our youth into the military and are especially upset that the armed forces are appropriating our cultural teachings, symbols, and music in order to do so.

First Nations people endured unique hardships during their service as they often faced racism and unequal treatment from their fellow servicemen. This unfair treatment continued when they returned home as many were denied veterans' benefits or were not made aware of those that they were entitled to for their service to Canada. While all veterans were supposed to receive access to land, education, grants, loans, and allowances for themselves and their children, many First Nations veterans were denied the full benefits. Of those who received benefits, most receive less than half of what non-First Nations veterans received in veterans' allowance; First Nations women were often denied their husband's benefits for their children as Indian agents did not believe that they would be able to handle money, and while non-First Nations veterans were able to acquire and own land, First Nations veterans were often only allowed to farm reserve land, but not own it. Some veterans had to give up their Indian status in order to serve in the military, so they were unable to return to their community where their families, traditional foods, and community supports were. Rather, many had to settle in unfamiliar towns where they faced racism that led to unemployment, poverty, and isolation which in turn sometimes led to substance abuse and/or suicide as a way to escape from their harsh reality.

The unequal and unjust treatment of First Nations veterans gained national headlines in 2002 when the Government of Canada finally offered compensation to First Nations veterans for their loss of benefits. The Saskatchewan First Nations Veterans Association (SFNVA) and the Assembly of First Nations (AFN) lobbied for justice for First Nations veterans for many years. The federal government's response was to offer a small token to those who served in the World War Two and the Korean War. The $20,000 maximum allocation to qualified veterans is a long way from Veterans Affairs Canada and the SFNVA's suggested compensation of $120,000 to each First Nations veteran. Chiefs at the AFN 2008 General Assembly renewed their partnership with the SFNVA and efforts to have the Government of Canada fully resolve outstanding injustices towards First Nations veterans.

Today, many more people are becoming aware of the great sacrifices that First Nations veterans made in order to serve a country that did a great disservice to them in return. Filmmakers, writers, and community organizers are finding ways to honor First Nations veterans at the community and national level. Their efforts include highlighting the outstanding contributions that First Nations veterans made as scouts, snipers, leaders, and code talkers. Loretta Todd was among the first to document veterans stories in 1997 with *Forgotten Warriors*, the famous Navajo code talkers were honored in the 2002 major motion picture *Wind Talkers* for their outstanding contributions to allied forces as no one was able to break their Navajo language code, and in his 2005 book *Three Day Road*, Joseph Boyden made real for us what it was like for a First Nations person to be in a war. After many years of advocacy and fundraising by National Aboriginal Veterans Associations, the First Nations Veterans Monument was unveiled in Ottawa in 2001. In addition, the SFNVA fundraised and advocated for the glass First Nations Veterans Memorial Tipi that was built into the main entrance of the First Nations University of Canada in Regina. Many communities across the country also acknowledge Aboriginal Veterans Day on November 8.

Find Out More

Forgotten Warriors. Loretta Todd. National Film Board of Canada. 1997.
Riverside National Cemetery in California.
Three Day Road. Joseph Boyden. Penguin Books. 2005.
National Native American Veterans Association.
Native Soldiers - Foreign Battlefields. Veterans Affairs Canada.
Aboriginal Veterans Essential Facts & Time Line. The War Amps.

Women – 500 Missing and Murdered

That's right, 500 missing and murdered First Nations women in Canada. Up until a few years ago, there was very little attention paid to this reality by mainstream media or even our First Nations leadership, except for the Native Women's Association of Canada (NWAC) who has been successful in raising awareness of the First Nations women missing or murdered across Canada. NWAC was an informant for Amnesty International's 2004 Stolen Sisters report which notes that decades of government policy were major contributors to putting First Nations women at great risk for acts of violence that sometimes also led to their premature death. The report also highlights the inaction of police authorities across the country in relation to missing, brutalized, and murdered First Nations women. While most people still use the figure of 500, NWAC now estimates the number of missing and murdered First Nations women to be closer to 600 and it is widely acknowledged that we do not know the true extent of the issue. What we do know is that our women continue to go missing or are murdered without much attention being paid by police or the mainstream media.

It is a true shame for Canada that the lives of First Nations mothers, daughters, nieces, aunts, and grandmothers are valued less than non-First Nations women's lives. There are those who say this is untrue, but actions speak louder than words. Until the day comes when it is common for a police officer to take serious a report of a missing First Nations woman, when it is common for police and the justice system to vigorously pursue and prosecute those who abuse and murder our women, when First Nations leaders view, prioritize, and act on this important issue, and when our communities actively work to stop violence in our communities, it will continue to be clear that First Nations women's lives have far less value than anyone else's.

"Some of their stories reveal experiences of poverty, abuse or addictions ...[but] many of these women and girls were 'vulnerable' only insofar as they were Aboriginal women ...it was assumed that either they would not fight back or they would not be missed."

Native Women's Association of Canada. 2010

It was no surprise to First Nations women when it became clear that the majority of women missing and murdered from Vancouver's Downtown Eastside were First Nations. The same is true for the Highway of Tears between Prince George and Terrace, B.C. where mostly First Nations women continue to go missing or turn up murdered. It was also no surprise to hear that for literally years, many community members reported to police that women were missing but the police did little to nothing about it until it became very public and therefore something they could no longer ignore. Even to this day, police will not readily admit that it is an attack on our women even though the majority are First Nations women.

The Women's Memorial March Committee in Vancouver, B.C. has been at the forefront of this issue for the past 20 years. Among other things, they lead a yearly Valentine's Day march through the streets of Vancouver's Downtown Eastside that stops at sites where missing women were last seen or found. Their work has garnered national and international attention in recent years. NWAC's campaigns have brought the issue of missing and murdered First Nations women to light. Without their hard work, there would be no national vigils, very little support to the missing women's families, no federal government action, and no national media coverage. NWAC's five-year effort resulted in the release of *What Their Stories Tell Us*, which highlights the gaps in knowledge that inhibit the development of effective policies and programs that can help to reduce violence against First Nations women, amongst other things. However, despite this great success and public statements by federal officials that they would further support the Sisters In Spirit Initiative, that was not the case. Rather, the federal government publicly surprised NWAC in late 2010 by announcing that the $10 million that was discussed would go to policing and other initiatives rather than to NWAC to continue their important work. After generating much public awareness, NWAC was able to secure some funding to start Evidence to Action II which will focus on education and resources to help raise awareness about violence. However, the funding does not allow NWAC to continue to use the 'Sisters In Spirit' name or NWAC's work on the database of missing First Nations women.

There is lots of talk by the Government of Canada and some provinces about reconciliation, but what does that really mean in the day-to-day lives of First Nations women? It is clear that government policies and actions have severely deteriorated our lives and communities. We face many social issues that leave us at risk of being exploited, abused, and murdered. Until the day comes when the Government of Canada is decent enough to begin to provide meaningful opportunities for us to recover from centuries of assimilation policies that have led to our women going missing and being murdered, there will be no real change.

Find Out More

Women's Memorial March – Vancouver, B.C.
20th Annual Women's Memorial March (Unceded Coast Salish Territory) Feb 14/2011 (Youtube video)
Survival, Strength, Sisterhood: Power of Women in the Downtown Eastside. Alejandro Zuluaga. 2011.
Sisters In Spirit. Native Women's Association of Canada.
Finding Dawn Documentary. Christine Welsh. National Film Board of Canada. 2006.
What Their Stories Tell Us: Research findings from the Sisters In Spirit initiative. Native Women's Association of Canada. 2010.
The sad fate of too many native women (article). Carol Goar. thestar.com. May 20, 2009.

Justice Issues

First Nations people are over-represented in all aspects of the justice system including stops by police, arrests, charges, remand, incarceration, women in solitary confinement, deaths in custody, federal sentences, and a lack of access to parole or release. The unique experience of First Nations people's conflict with the justice system is well-documented by the federal government, advocacy groups, and First Nations political organizations. The Office of the Corrections Investigator (OCI), the Canadian Association of Elizabeth Fry Societies (CAEFS) and many others point to the multi-generational effects of governmental assimilation policies as key contributors to the over-representation of First Nations people throughout the criminal justice system. There are various initiatives across the country to address some of these issues, but not nearly enough to make the systemic change that is needed for First Nations people to have the same uninhibited access to justice that others do. Some of the initiatives include police and First Nations community relations, restorative or transformative justice which includes sentencing circles, the right to practice cultural ceremonies in prisons, and courts that are more culturally appropriate such as the Tsuu T'ina First Nation Court, the Cree-speaking Circuit Court, and the urban Gladue Court. The majority of these initiatives were only developed after years of advocacy and pressure from the First Nations community. The OCI's 2009 *Good Intentions, Disappointing Results: A Progress Report on Federal Aboriginal Corrections* reported that there had been little progress made over the previous 10 years in correctional outcomes for First Nations people. The OCI notes that "Aboriginal corrections is at a crossroads in Canada, with a need for urgent action on the part of the [Corrections Services Canada] absent which the situation may devolve into crisis" that will negatively affect all Canadians, not just First Nations people.

CAEFS' 2005 submission to the United Nations Human

Rights Committee highlighted many of the human rights violations against First Nations women within Correctional Services of Canada. CAEFS noted that the "depth and degree of systemic discrimination experienced by Aboriginal women means they are more likely than are non-Aboriginal women to have criminal records and to have previously experienced prison", that they tend to be segregated more often and longer, and that "as prisoners, Aboriginal women suffer the compounded disadvantages of being both women and Aboriginal prisoners in a discriminatory correctional system." Additionally, the B.C. Civil Liberties Association (BCCLA) filed a complaint in March 2011 on behalf of a First Nations woman who has spent almost her entire sentence on the Management Protocol which allows for continuous segregation/solitary confinement of women. Only seven women have been on the protocol, which has been slammed by human rights groups since it was introduced in 2005. In March 2011, all women suffering from this barbaric practice were First Nations women leading the BCCLA to question whether the practice was being applied in a discriminatory manner.

While First Nations people work toward being healthier individuals, families, and communities, there are still many who are living lives steeped in confusion, anger, addiction, poverty, silence, and shame from the inter-generational effects of assimilation policies. For many, their coping mechanisms make it more likely that they will come into conflict with a justice system that does not understand their realities, or sometimes seems to not even value us as human beings as was witnessed in the death of Frank Paul in Vancouver. Others who are living in poverty, especially women, may end up with a criminal record for stealing food or diapers for their children. There are significant barriers at all levels of the criminal justice system that can lead to a First Nations person becoming yet another statistic. Things that can lead a First Nations person right into a jail cell include racism within policing departments and criminal profiling which lead to First Nations people being stopped and charged with a crime at high rates, whether or not they committed the crime; the extreme poverty in our communities can lead to criminal activity that might not otherwise happen such as being forced into the sex trade or stealing food for children; and social conditions that continue due to the failure by the Government of Canada to help reverse the inter-generational issues that have been created by government policy. Once charged with a crime, First Nations people often face multiple barriers that do not allow them to meaningfully understand their legal options in relation to seeking legal counsel or getting bail. Issues that might find someone pleading guilty to a crime, when they might not otherwise, include having English as a second language (if at all), not having someone to adequately explain to them what all of their options are, not wanting to stay in jail while they wait for a judge to come to their community for their monthly visit, not understanding how the justice system works, not understanding how a criminal record might negatively affect their future aspirations, amongst others. These barriers can lead to decisions being made that will likely snowball over their lifetime, including spending lengthier jail sentences in the future.

Systemic racism issues within the criminal justice system result in First Nations people being more likely to be convicted of a crime, to be sentenced to longer terms, to be denied their cultural and religious freedoms, and to be transferred away from their home communities and, therefore, their support systems. First Nations groups assert that First Nations' religious freedom is often infringed when Directive 702, which is a health directive regarding exposure to second-hand smoke, is used to deny or restrict First Nations' ceremonial practices of burning medicines such as sweetgrass, sage, or other medicines within correctional facilities. Many people believe that Directive 702 is used to deny us our rights to practice our own religion or spirituality by those who do not understand and/or value its inherent benefits in helping individuals to overcome the barriers, situations, or circumstances that led them to prison. Many First Nations inmates have their first exposure to First Nations traditions and ceremonies in jail. These individuals are often profoundly touched and changed for the better from learning about and practicing their culture. First Nations justice advocates believe that the best way to rehabilitate First Nations inmates is by introducing them to their cultural traditions as a way of helping them to build their pride and self-esteem as a First Nations person and therefore to be better equipped to handle the daily stresses and challenges that may lead them into conflict with the justice system.

Stemming the Tide – Partnerships with First Nations

There are a few federal, provincial, and territorial initiatives that are helping to stem the tide of First Nations victimization, crime, and incarceration. These programs have been developed in recognition that First Nations communities and culture must be included in justice initiatives if there is to be any real and sustainable change. While there is still lots of room for improvement, the following are initiatives with great promise which may be realized if there is meaningful input, direction, and implementation by First Nations communities.

- The Federal Aboriginal Justice Strategy's Community-based Justice Programs and Capacity Building Funds provide funding to First Nations communities to help reduce victimization, crime, and incarceration through culturally appropriate community-based intervention models such as sentencing circles, alternative sentencing measures, family and civil mediation, offender-reintegration, and victim support, among others.
- Healing Lodges have been established to better meet the needs of First Nations inmates by providing culturally appropriate programs, settings, and staff; levels of each vary at each lodge. Eight lodges have been established in mostly rural settings, only one is for women, and some continue to be operated by Corrections Services Canada, rather than a First Nations community.

- The Aboriginal Courtworker Program helps First Nations individuals to understand their rights and options, and works with justice officials to help them to better understand and meet the needs of First Nations people.
- The Gladue Court in Toronto is a dedicated courtroom with judges, lawyers, prosecutors, and case workers trained to better meet the needs of First Nations people as per Section 718.2(e) of the *Criminal Code* of Canada which calls for all alternatives to be considered before imprisonment. A Gladue Report is prepared with recommendations for alternative measures which are based on interviews and research on the history of the accused that may have led them into conflict with the law.
- First Nations Policing – There are 405 First Nations communities with dedicated police services employing over 1,200 First Nations officers. Services are either self-administered by First Nations communities or are managed through the Royal Canadian Mounted Police.

The implementation of culturally appropriate and community-based initiatives are very important in helping to reduce First Nations' victimization, criminal activity, and incarceration, but they are only one part of the answer. There must be many more prevention-based initiatives developed and administered in partnership with First Nations people before there will be a significant change. The best way to stem the tide that leaves First Nations people more likely to go to jail than to graduate high school is to implement First Nations people's recommendations on how to holistically address these problems. Recommendations include addressing the inter-generational social and economic effects of colonization and the residential school experiences, re-establishing traditional justice practices such as sentencing circles, eliminating racism from the criminal justice system, having on-reserve policing based on First Nations beliefs and customs, and reversing the overwhelming poverty in First Nations communities by providing meaningful access to culturally appropriate education, training, and employment programs in areas where First Nations people live.

Incarceration Statistics

- The higher rate of incarceration for First Nations peoples has been linked to systemic discrimination and attitudes based on racial or cultural prejudice, as well as economic and social deprivation, substance abuse and a cycle of violence across generations
- First Nations make up only 2.7% of the adult population, but almost 18.5% of those serving federal sentences.
- First Nations people's over-representation is worst in the west. In the Prairies, where First Nations people make up a large part of the population, 60 percent of those incarcerated are First Nations.
- First Nations women are even more over-represented at 30% than Aboriginal men in federal prisons.
- The federally incarcerated population in Canada declined by 12.5% from 1996 to 2004, while First Nations people increased by 21%, with women increasing by 74.2%

(Statistics above from Office of the Correctional Investigator)

- Employment and education characteristics of young Aboriginal adults explain about half of their over-representation in custody in 2007/2008
- In 2007-2008, 17.3% of the total federal offender population was Aboriginal compared to being 4% of the Canadian adult population. They represented 19.6% of those incarcerated and 13.6% of those on conditional release (parole).

(Statistics above are from Statistics Canada)

Find Out More

The incarceration of Aboriginal people in adult correctional services. Samuel Perreault. Juristat. Vol. 29, no. 3. July 2009.
Aboriginal Courts in Canada Fact Sheet. Scow Institute. 2008.
Submission of the Canadian Association of Elizabeth Fry Societies to the United Nations Human Rights Committee Examining Canada's 5th Report Regarding the International Covenant on Civil and Political Rights. September 2005.
Good Intentions, Disappointing Results: A Progress Report on Federal Aboriginal Corrections. Office of the Corrections Investigator. 2009.
First Nations Chiefs of Police Association
First Nations Policing Policy. Government of Canada. 2006.

Human Rights

One would naturally assume that all people in Canada enjoy the same human rights, but unfortunately for First Nations people this is not so. We are governed by the *Indian Act* which still contains sections that are discriminatory against women in particular. Legislation such as the *Canadian Human Rights Act* is also impacted by the *Indian Act*. The Government of Canada is correct in its assertion that they have made repeated attempts to change both pieces of legislation; however, their approach has delayed the changes far beyond what is necessary. While it seems that this is a straightforward matter, for First Nations people it is not. The repeal or change of any legislation must be considered along with the duty to consult with First Nations people, First Nations inherent rights, treaty rights, First Nation sovereignty, and First Nations laws. Until the Government of Canada is willing to seriously work towards finding common ground in this work, many First Nations people will continue to suffer needlessly while the Government of Canada continues to implement its assimilationist policies which they believe and assert are in our best interest.

One significant area that is lacking is matrimonial real property rights which cover the on-reserve land and house that are related to a common-law or married couple. Currently, when an on-reserve relationship dissolves, there is no legal remedy for dividing up real property so women and their children may find themselves evicted from their home with nowhere to go. The Native Women's Association of Canada (NWAC) worked in good faith with the Government of Canada on nation-wide consultations that resulted the report *Matrimonial Real Property: A People's Report* which was submitted to the Government of Canada to ensure they would consider how to redress this issue. NWAC has made clear to the federal government that instituting the same or similar laws that apply to all matrimonial property in Canada is not sufficient as people who live on-reserve are governed under other legislation which does not easily transfer.

Even the *Indian Act* does not address this important issue, so on-reserve First Nations women continue to be left to essentially fend for themselves. The Ministerial Representative submitted her separate report in March, 2007. The Government of Canada has asserted its autonomous legislative authority to remedy this huge problem by choosing to ignore NWAC's report which represented the voice of thousands of First Nations women, Elders, and other community members from across the country. Despite NWAC's non-endorsement of the legislation, the Government of Canada tabled *The Family Homes on Reserve and Matrimonial Interests or Rights Act*, which is currently working its way through the parliamentary process. This blatant disregard for First Nations people's input is yet another example of meaningless consultations carried out by the Government of Canada. Until this archaic piece of legislation is replaced with something that First Nations people believe can help to rebuild our communities, while still holding the Government of Canada to their fiduciary responsibilities to First Nations people, there will continue to be human rights violations against our people which are legally sanctioned by the Government of Canada.

Another significant legislative gap is related to section Section 67 of the *Canadian Human Rights Act* (*CHRA*) which cannot contravene any provision made under or pursuant to the *Indian Act*. This Section severely limits First Nations people's right to utilize the *CHRA*. The courts are able to hear some complaints, but not if the matter is related to the *Indian Act*. The only First Nations that are subject to the *CHRA* are self-governing First Nations that have opted out of the *Indian Act*. The federal government and First Nations people have very different views on how to implement the *CHRA* on-reserve. First Nations are worried about inherent individual and collective treaty and First Nations rights being trampled upon while the federal government insists on pushing their remedy through without first addressing First Nations' concerns.

Find Out More

First Nations Perspectives on Bill C-44 (Repeal of Section 67 of Canadian Human Rights Act). Assembly of First Nations. 2007.
Open Letter to the Government of Canada on the U.N. Declaration. Native Women's Association of Canada. 2008.
Matrimonial Real Property Consultations: An Information Kit. Native Women's Association of Canada. 2006.
Matrimonial Real Property: A People's Report. Native Women's Association of Canada. 2006.
Family Homes on Reserves and Matrimonial Interests or Rights Act. Library of Parliament. Government of Canada. 2010.

Sidebar – International Shame

The most recent attempt to ignore the inherent rights of First Nations people came in 2007 when Canada joined the United States, New Zealand, and Australia as one of only four countries to vote against the *United Nations Declaration on the Rights of Indigenous Peoples*. In May 2008, over 100 legal experts released an open letter urging the Government of Canada to stop disseminating erroneous information about the Declaration and to fulfill its promise to sign it. They stated that the *Declaration* is consistent with the *Canadian Constitution* and *Charter of Rights and Freedoms* and that "Government claims to the contrary do a grave disservice to the cause of human rights and to the promotion of harmonious and cooperative relations". Australia finally signed on in 2009; New Zealand endorsed it in 2010; and the United States is leading Native Americans to believe that they will also sign. Canada dragged its heels until finally being shamed into signing it in December 2010. However, the Minister of Indian Affairs was quick to refer to the Declaration as an *aspirational* document that it is not legally binding.

Post-Residential School Era

The negative effects of the residential school system in Canada have been well-documented and acknowledged by many, including the Government of Canada and the churches that operated the schools. Despite many reports, books, and efforts by First Nations people and their allies, it took decades of pressure from the First Nations community before the Government of Canada finally made a formal public apology in June 2008 to residential school survivors. While standing in the Parliament of Canada in a nationally televised address, the Prime Minister acknowledged the many abuses that First Nations children were forced to experience and how that reality still negatively affects the lives of First Nations people today. In addition, after many years of negotiations with the Assembly of First Nations, the Government of Canada began sending out compensation cheques to residential school survivors across Canada who could prove that they went to a residential school and for how long. If they can prove they were a student, they must then file a formal claim even if they cannot read or write. In recognition that every person who went to residential school suffered some form of abuse and loss, the Government of Canada agreed to pay a Common Experience Payment of $10,000 plus $3,000 for each year that a survivor spent in a residential school. Each person can then also file a separate claim for specific abuses or losses if they choose. There are additional ways to opt in or out of other processes, including taking legal action.

Although there is now compensation for those who can prove they attended residential schools, there has been no agreement reached for the thousands of individuals who attended Indian Day Schools. Approximately 70,000 First Nations children attended day schools. The Spiritwind Society notes that day school attendees suffered the same types of abuses as those who attended and lived in residential schools. The main difference being that they were able to go home at night. In order to seek the same recognition, apology, and compensation that residential school survivors received, a $15 billion class action lawsuit was filed by lawyer Joan Jack in 2009 to gain compensation for those who attended day schools.

During the many years that it has taken First Nations people to force the Government of Canada to formally and publicly apologize and financially compensate survivors of the residential school system, many of our Elders have died without the benefit of knowing that the Government of Canada was in a small way acknowledging that what they did was morally wrong and that the children who attended these institutions suffered life-altering abuse. There are still others who suffered from their experience at residential schools or the inter-generational effects of the residential school experience who lived a life of pain, addiction, and loneliness and who have since died an unnatural and early death due to their suffering which was often masked in their addictions.

An important component of the residential schools settlement agreement was the establishment of the Indian Residential School Truth and Reconciliation Commission (TRC) to work towards truth, healing, and reconciliation regarding the residential school experience. The TRC was formed as a result of the terms negotiated by survivors who wanted to ensure that their experiences were never forgotten or repeated. The TRC's goals include providing a safe and supportive space for residential school survivors to tell their story; to document the history of residential schools, its impacts, and survivor's stories to preserve them for historical and learning purposes; and to help foster reconciliation. After a false start in 2008 due to internal bickering and posturing over who had authority to do what, the TRC began its important work in 2009. During this delay, many survivors died without having the opportunity to tell their stories. The TRC will also look into the death of children connected to residential schools. The Missing Children and Unmarked Burials Research will seek to identify how many children died at residential schools and where they were buried. The Aboriginal Healing Foundation's initial research into this area ran into many hurdles including incomplete church and government documents, and notations about a death without any further information about how and when a child died or where they were buried. These hurdles will severely restrict efforts to identify the true number of lost lives of children in residential schools. The TRC hosted the first of seven national educational events in Winnipeg in the summer of 2010, and will host its northern national event in Inuvik, Northwest Territories in 2011.

It is important to note that all of the churches made a formal apology in some form in the 1990s, except the Roman Catholic Church. In April 2009, Pope Benedict XVI stated his "sorrow for the abuse and deplorable treatment that Aboriginal students suffered at Roman Catholic Church-run residential schools." That was not an apology. While each church has made some form of apology or statement, they are worded very carefully as to not open themselves up to lawsuits. It is very clear that they are looking after their own vested interests, rather than following their own religious teachings which would have them confess to their sins and make amends. Some of the churches are working in small ways with various First Nations people or communities to begin to make amends. I suggest that all of the churches who ran the schools come clean and confess their sins to First Nations people and their own followers. They all seem to be worried about opening themselves up to civil suits that could destroy their financial kingdoms. Why don't they ask their followers to contribute to a healing fund? Of course, they have already shown that they do not know what is best for First Nations people, so they should set up an endowment fund that First Nations people can administer and access to offer meaningful healing and cultural revival activities to survivors and their descendants.

The Prime Minister of Canada acknowledged in the apology to residential school survivors that "the legacy of Indian Residential Schools has contributed to social problems that continue to exist in many communities today" as the inter-generational effects continue to carry on. Some First Nations people have found a way to recover from this history, others have learned to just survive rather than thrive, but many others still suffer the individual and familial problems that stem from residential school abuses.

The next chapter of this terrible story is yet to be seen, but it is clear that the Government of Canada is not living up to its words in its apology to survivors. The Prime Minister of Canada may have made the formal apology to residential school survivors, but his government turned around and cut funding to the National Residential School Survivors Society and the Aboriginal Healing Foundation as of March 31, 2010. This sort of action is just one example of why First Nations people continue to doubt the sincerity of the apology or commitment to helping First Nations individual and communities overcome the inter-generational effects of the residential schools.

Find Out More

A Brief Report of The Federal Government of Canada's Residential School System for Inuit. David King. Aboriginal Healing Foundation. 2006.
Métis History and Experience and Residential Schools in Canada. Larry N. Chartrand, T. E. Logan, J.D. Daniels. Aboriginal Healing Foundation. 2006.
Directory of Residential Schools in Canada. Aboriginal Healing Foundation. Revised 2007.
Indian Residential Schools Settlement Agreement
Truth and Reconciliation Commission of Canada
Native American Policy Resolution. United States of America. 2009.
Where the Blood Mixes (play). Kevin Loring.
Government of Canada's Statement of Apology to Residential School Survivors (can be found in print or on Youtube)
Missing Children and Unmarked Burials: Research Recommendations. The Working Group on Missing Children & Unmarked Burials. 2008.

Sidebar – Everyone is Affected

One important missing piece in the whole residential school fallout is the acknowledgement of the negative effects that all Canadians bear. I only mention this point as many non-First Nations individuals will not understand how it affects them until it hits them in the wallet. When this is looked at from a purely economic lens, there are tens of thousands of people who have not had a meaningful opportunity to benefit from and contribute to Canada's economy. Rather, they struggle to lead healthy lives, and increase the social costs to all Canadians in terms of the justice system, welfare system, healthcare system, and many others. Therefore, it is important that all Canadians pressure the Government of Canada to truly address the legacy of their residential school fiasco.

While the then federal Liberal government hammered out the Kelowna Accord in 2005 with First Nations leaders, there was still no true acknowledgement of the work that needed to be done to address the underlying causes of poverty, addiction, and family break-up. If you ask the women of the community, you will likely get a different, more family-focused opinion that will help to make meaningful change for their families. It is great to have money, but if you are struggling with addiction you just have more money to spend on alcohol or drugs. Don't get me wrong, I think it is very important to address poverty and economic development, but these initiatives must be coupled with well-resourced, long-term initiatives that address the underlying issues that are the legacy of the residential schools.

Media

Over the past few decades as First Nations people have become more involved in multi-media, there has been the creation of First Nations media sources that can better represent our realities. There are now some local and regional newspapers, a growing number of extensive websites, some radio stations and shows which are mostly in the North where our population outnumbers non-First Nations people, and the Aboriginal People's Television Network (APTN) has been on mainstream cable for over a decade now. In fact, I am very happy to now see a few stories on the CTV network that were produced by APTN and have First Nations reporters on screen. These exciting developments help to ensure that a fuller extent of our realities are offered to the public, and not just the negative stuff that the vast majority of mainstream media seems to focus on.

As long as our oldest people can remember, mainstream media has directed its attention to negative stories about First Nations people. We are depicted primarily as victims, social problems, or warriors against mainstream society. More often than not, media stories are focused on inflammatory issues such as roadblocks, land claims, poor social conditions, tragedy, residential school abuses, or non-First Nations people protesting First Nations' fishing rights. Rarely do I see a positive story about First Nations people that is run just for the sake of running it, other than on APTN.

It seems that non-First Nations people have to benefit by what is happening before a story is considered newsworthy. A good example is when a treaty is signed in British Columbia. It is news because a treaty will provide certainty for multi-national and other large companies who are biting at the bit to extract natural resources from the area. It would be great to see positive stories that are happening in the First Nations community; after all, First Nations people also watch, listen to, and read the news. I'm sure the average citizen would be pleasantly surprised to learn about the good work that is being done in our communities in helping our families lead healthy lives, about First Nations cultural revival, National Aboriginal History Month, or about our young entrepreneurs, rather than mostly hearing about the doom and gloom of residential schools and suicides. Once the average person realizes that First Nations people's good health, living conditions, and settling of treaties and land claims positively affect all people, not just us, there will be more interest in our issues and concerns. Media should be a catalyst for this change in perspective, rather than just perpetuating narrow views about First Nations people.

Every year I anxiously wait to see if there will be more than a 15-second clip on National Aboriginal Day activities, if any coverage at all. Year after year, I am disappointed. At first one might consider that there is not much media coverage about National Aboriginal Day because it is not a national holiday. But when you look closer at the issue, you will be astounded by the fact that the news stations will run stories day-after-day about Chinese New Year or Diwali, which are also not national holidays, but will have few or no reports on National Aboriginal Day. It isn't difficult to conclude that the media just doesn't care enough to look for interesting stories during National Aboriginal Day. This lack of attention is a clear indication that there is not much change happening in mainstream media in relation to First Nations people. The media reports on things that they assume people want to hear, so they pay very little attention to First Nations people. I think this is selling non-First Nations people and the country short, as they do not get to see how much they can learn from us in relation to many issues including our spirituality, resilience, creative endeavours, or how to be good environmental caretakers. It wouldn't be hard to find interesting stories in the First Nations community - if the media cared enough to try.

Find Out More

Aboriginal People's Television Network National News
Turtle Island Native Network Website
Indian Country Today (U.S. National Newspaper)
Nunatsiaq News (news from Nunavut)
From the Tomahawk Chop to the Road Block: Discourses of Savagism in Whitestream Media. Daniel Morley Johnson. American Indian Quarterly - Volume 35, Number 1, Winter 2011, pp. 104-134.
The Media, Aboriginal People and Common Sense. Robert Harding. 2002.
National Coalition on Racism in Sport and the Media

Taxes – Do We Really Pay Them?

There are a few circumstances in which First Nations people can claim an *Indian Act* related tax exemption; moreover, no one is able to claim a tax exemption unless they are a Status Indian as defined by the Government of Canada (approximately 60% of First Nations population). Most Métis and Inuit people are not eligible for these tax exemptions unless they have Indian status through their lineage or marriage. Laws related to the taxation of Status Indians have their foundation in Section 87 of the *Indian Act.* Indian and Northern Affairs Canada notes that First Nations tax law "reflects the unique constitutional and historic place of Aboriginal people in Canada." These rights have been upheld by courts which affirm that "the exemption is intended to preserve the entitlements of Indian people to their reserve lands, and to ensure that the use of their property on their reserve lands is not eroded by taxation." Two of the most common areas that Status Indians can claim a tax exemption are for personal income tax and the purchasing of goods and services; both of which must have direct connections to a First Nations reserve.

The Government of Canada has developed a number of connecting factors that must be present before an individual is eligible for a personal income tax exemption for all or part of their personal earnings. The most important questions are if they are a Status Indian, if they work on a reserve, if they do work that benefits those living on a reserve, if their employer is on-reserve, and if they themselves live on a reserve. Any exemption would require various combinations of these factors and possibly others to support a person's legal right to claim an income tax exemption. Relatively few people are able to claim this exemption due to low employment on reserves.

Status Indians may also claim a tax exemption for goods or services if they are purchased on a reserve. Given that approximately 60% of all First Nations people now live off-reserve, the remoteness of many reserves, and the low number of reserve-based businesses, there are not large amounts of people making purchases on reserve. Status Indians can also have items delivered onto their reserve to claim the tax exemption. However, some businesses refuse to comply with the *Income Tax Act* and force Status Indians to pay the taxes and go through the lengthy process of claiming the taxes back from the government themselves. Since many Status Indians who live on reserve or in remote areas do not have access to a range of businesses, they are often forced to go through this uncalled for inconvenience in order to meet some of their basic needs.

The signing of modern day treaties is adding to the diversity of tax-related experience for Status Indians as recent treaties have provisions regarding *Indian Act*-related taxation. Most have a gradual implementation of rules that will lead to the loss of purchase of goods or services and personal income tax exemptions. Some treaties also enable a First Nations Band to implement property taxes on-reserve, similar to how a municipality does. Most of this change is happening in British Columbia where less than 5% of the land is covered by a treaty. In other areas of the country, some land claims agreements and other negotiations have led to Bands gaining the authority to tax various items purchased on-reserve. These actions are being taken to help individual Bands build an economic base to support the needs of their members. It is anticipated that the federal and provincial governments will continue to push for full taxation of Status Indians, and First Nations leadership will fight to retain this right.

<u>Find Out More</u>

Indian & Northern Affairs Canada FAQ Sheet on Taxes
Modern Treaties and Taxation. Indian & Northern Affairs Canada.
Aboriginal People and Taxation. Elaine Gardner-O'Toole. Law and Government Division. 1992.
Status Indians and Taxes. Indian and Northern Affairs Canada. 2002.

Free Stuff – What Do We Really Get For "Free"?

Many people have at some point believed that First Nations people get most things for free; however, this not true. More people are becoming aware of the reality of our lives, but for the most part we still fight against the misperception that we are 'free loaders'. The most common assumptions are about fishing, land ownership, taxes, housing, education, and healthcare; all which may be available to some individuals, but only if they have Indian status. An Indian status number and card is official recognition by the Government of Canada that a person is a 'real' First Nations person who has not lost their inherent rights through various means such as marriage to a non-status person.

Before I go down the fictitious resource rich path, I want to talk about this notion of things being obtained for 'free'. The founding fathers of what is now known as Canada signed agreements to provide certain things in exchange for the millions and millions and millions of acres of land that they took over after they came here. That is the first truth that most don't know about or choose to forget or ignore. If the Government of Canada even remotely met their obligations under those agreements, all Status Indians would have a bit of land, a medicine chest, free education, access to their traditional territories and foods, or many other things depending on which treaty they were associated with. It is not our fault that these men did not have the foresight to realize that they could not make us disappear either through killing us or by assimilating us. It is more than a bit funny that a government that is so focused on the economy, business, and the justice system, is not able to hold itself to high standards when it comes to First Nations people. Shame on them.

I will only provide one example here as you can find out about taxes, education, and housing in those sections of this book. Sure, when they said we would forever have a medicine chest, they didn't think that it would be so huge now. One might be tempted to ask why the government should pay for a full medicine chest when times have changed and First Nations people need to take responsibility for their own health. Of the many reasons I could state, three are most important. One, they signed the agreement. Two, the government is responsible for a free market system that has led to the overall decline in all people's health. And three, their ongoing assimilationist policies have led to First Nations people's declining physical, mental, emotional, and spiritual health. But despite all of these reasonable facts, the Government of Canada continues to decrease our health benefits.

Sidebar – Status Indians?

Words such as 'status' and 'reserves' are usually associated with prosperity and social status, which is not the case for First Nations people. By design or not, these words help to take away some of the negativity of our reality and must have some effect on the perceptions of those who do not truly understand our day-to-day reality. Someone in mainstream society may gain status by being born into the right family, but you surely don't gain any status in Canada by being born a First Nations person.

Appropriate Questions to Ask A First Nations Person

Many First Nations people appreciate being asked thoughtful questions by people who genuinely want to learn more about our culture, traditions, and history. However, it becomes quite frustrating as a First Nations person to be continually asked about First Nation issues as if we are the only means to find the information. This is especially true when we are asked ignorant questions or ones that are based on hot button topics only. Many people expect First Nations individuals to be an open book and an expert on all there is to know about First Nations people. However, as you will learn from reading this book, there are so many issues that it is almost impossible to be able to have meaningful knowledge about everything. We aren't born knowing it, and our experiences over the past few hundred years leave us much less likely to know even a small portion of this information. No one expects the average non-First Nations person to know everything about all mainstream issues. Most cannot even tell you who the Prime Minister is, the names of five First Nations, what the true history of North America is, why unions set up their own types of roadblocks, what government policies are helping to collapse the salmon industry, how little tax big corporations pay, or where Christopher Columbus was really heading when he got lost and supposedly discovered a land that was already inhabited by millions of First Nations people.

There are few things more maddening than someone asking 'why are they setting up that roadblock', 'do you have lots of salmon', or 'do you pay taxes'. In reality, these are most often stated as a statement or accusation rather than a question. There is always a bit of bitterness in the person's tone which is likely due to their assumption that we are in competition for something with them or that we get something they don't. Rather than learn about the bigger systemic issues at play, they want to take out their frustration and aggression against any non-threatening First Nations person they run into. They often pose the question like they are curious, but often they are looking for a debate or someone to complain to about the issue. First Nations people are forced to react to government policy; we do not create them. So it does little good to complain to us about it.

Overall, those of us who are willing to have a discussion with strangers, classmates, or co-workers about our issues are more interested in answering questions that show you have a genuine interest in understanding our true history as the First People of North America, our uniqueness, our strengths, where you might be able to do your own research, and how you might be able to help foster positive change for First Nations people. Those are the types of questions that I welcome.

Find Out More

Revision Quest. Darrell Dennis. CBC Radio.

INHERENT RIGHTS

TREATIES PLUS MILLIONS AND MILLIONS OF ACRES OF LAND

EQUALS DOWN PAYMENT ON FUTURE GENERATION'S HEALTH, EDUCATION, SELF-GOVERNANCE, HUNTING, GATHERING, AND ALL OTHER INHERENT RIGHTS!

lyndatoon

Chapter 5

Health & Wellness

Increasing numbers of First Nations people are focusing on healing and wellness for themselves and their families. As more of us begin to understand our past, we are able to look hopefully toward the future. Many individuals and organizations are helping to break the silence so that true holistic healing and wellness can be achieved. The day that I learned the truth about the past few hundred years for First Nations people, I began to understand how my family and community came to be facing many of the social challenges that we are today. I felt truly empowered, not shamed. I understood that it was not our 'fault' that we face a myriad of health and social problems, that there was nothing wrong with us as a people, and that we could do something about it. This access to the truth is helping many others to understand that First Nations people are not meant to be facing challenges and they, as individuals, have the power to make positive changes in their own lives.

First Nations people are now learning and reclaiming our cultural traditions as a means of finding our place in the world, to honor our ancestors, and to work toward true healing. Many of our traditional ways included rituals that mark milestones such as puberty, marriage, and death. These rituals help us to learn the skills needed to take on these responsibilities and to cope with loss and trauma in a healthy way. We are relearning our healing ceremonies, utilizing sharing circles to share and honor each other's stories, incorporating cultural practices into our programs and services, and some communities are hosting culturally-focused healing camps.

Increasing numbers are learning that health is holistic, not just based on our physical needs. For instance, many people are now recognizing that our physical and emotional health can be greatly improved at a much faster rate through the teaching of cultural beliefs, practices, ceremonies, and other life skills that positively affect our emotional health. I refer to this as 'culture as therapy' as I have repeatedly witnessed the healing power that culture has for our people.

Michael Chandler and Chris Lalonde's research bears out the importance of addressing various issues to make needed improvements. Their work highlights community factors that influence individual life-affirming hopes including the community's level of self-governance, court action for land title, extent of local control over health, education, and policing, facilities for the preservation of culture, local control over child welfare services, and the extent to which women are in leadership roles. The greater number of these indicators, and at a higher level, that a community can achieve is likely to greatly reduce levels of depression and the number of suicides in that community, especially amongst youth. As more of these positive steps are achieved and people are incorporating the teachings of the medicine wheel into their lives, the faster we will see overall improvements in healing and wellness for individuals, families, and communities.

Spotlight – Mental Health

In 2006, the Senate Committee on Social Affairs acknowledged that First Nation people do not suffer from high rates of organic mental illness. Rather, many of our mental health concerns are brought on by external stressors which lead to high levels of anger, depression, stress, and suicide. Although many of us face these issues, we should be heartened that these are all reversible as they are not organic brain issues such as schizophrenia or dementia. In order to reach more people, some programs have changed their names, as the term 'mental health' is a barrier to service as it raises negative thoughts about the program and those who access it because some people relate it to being 'crazy' or 'mentally ill', not depressed or stressed.

Find Out More
Aboriginal Healing in Canada: Studies in Therapeutic Meaning and Practice. The Aboriginal Healing Foundation. 2008.
Cultural Continuity As A Protective Factor Against Suicide in First Nations Youth. Michael Chandler and Chris Lalonde. 2008.
First Nations Traditional Models of Wellness, Traditional Medicines and Practices: Environmental Scan in British Columbia. First Nations Healthy Society. 2010.
Introduction to the Medicine Wheel Concept. Kakakaway & Associates.
Urban First Nations Health Research Discussion Paper. National Aboriginal Health Organization. 2009.
Medicine Woman. Vision Television. 2007.

Medicine Wheel

The medicine wheel is not a concept that spans across all First Nations; however, most First Nations people have now come to believe in its teachings and accept it as a pan-First Nations belief as it includes many teachings that are common amongst most First Nations people.

The medicine wheel helps us to visualize and verbalize our beliefs in relation to our overall health. It encompasses countless teachings that I do not have the knowledge or right to share publicly. The basic teachings of the medicine wheel are widely known and can be shared here. The most significant teaching for me is that we are all made up of four areas: our physical, mental, emotional, and spiritual selves. It is believed that you must be balanced in all four areas to be truly healthy, happy, fulfilled, and balanced. The main colors of the medicine wheel are red, black, white, and yellow which represent many different teachings and are arranged in different order by different First Nations people. You may sometimes see medicine wheels that use blue instead of black as that is particular to certain Nations. The straight lines that section the circle into four quadrants represent the four directions and the start or ending of seasons or phases of life. The circle represents the holistic nature of the medicine wheel, life, and First Nations teachings. Those who utilize the medicine wheel will often draw it out and list things in each area to visually represent what they are doing in that area. This makes it easier to see deficiencies or excesses in each area. The person would then list things that they could incorporate into their lives to make themselves more balanced in all areas. Those who regularly utilize the medicine wheel find that it helps them to be more self-reflective, honest with themselves, focused, balanced, and healthy overall. The medicine wheel is most helpful when we refer to it regularly to assess our health and progress; it is not meant to be used once then put away where it can be easily forgotten. So someone like me, who works a lot, but does not put as much effort into their physical health is thought to be imbalanced - so therefore, not truly healthy. I can attest that it is true. It helps to know that neglecting this area has a negative effect on my overall health as I then tend to take it more seriously and try to do something about it.

The medicine wheel can be one of the most significant tools on First Nations people's road to recovery from many of the social challenges that we face today. A quick internet search will turn up references to work being done in the areas of health, child welfare, education, and other areas that require a holistic approach to become more effective and relevant to First Nations people. First Nations families and communities can utilize the medicine wheel teachings as a way to assess their overall health as a group. Is the family or community getting enough healthy food, are there enough physical activities for everyone, are there enough learning opportunities for everyone, are there counsellors to help people through their challenges, and are there opportunities for people to learn and practice spirituality? We can utilize the medicine wheel in creative ways that help us to take a realistic look at many things, so that we can work towards meaningful changes.

Large constructed wheels that have been found in various locations across North America are usually referred to as medicine wheels and are known to be created by First Nations people thousands of years ago. These circular sites are usually created in various forms from rocks and other natural items and are thought to be used for ceremonial and astrological purposes, amongst other things. The sacred sites are a curiosity to tourists and anthropologists alike who struggle to find modern day meaning in an ancient practice and site that is not meant to be understood or accessed by all. Meanwhile, First Nations people fight to preserve the sites which have become a beacon of hope for many.

Find Out More

Introduction to the Medicine Wheel Concept. Kakakaway & Associates.

Aboriginal Healing in Canada: Studies in Therapeutic Meaning and Practice. The Aboriginal Healing Foundation. 2008.

The Circle of Courage Philosophy. Reclaiming Youth International.

Spotlight – The Circle of Courage

Reclaiming Youth International developed the Circle of Courage model as a cross-cultural tool to help reclaim at-risk youth back into their communities. The model incorporates the holistic wellness model of the medicine wheel as a means to convey the importance of teaching community members that the answers to many social problems facing youth today must be addressed from a community level for meaningful change to occur. Their Circle of Courage quadrants consist of belonging, mastery, independence, and generosity as the keys to helping youth gain courage to face life's challenges. Their model calls on all community members, schools, and others to help develop strong and healthy youth by recognizing both their challenges and strengths from which they can draw upon to make healthy decisions and change in their lives.

Traditional Medicines

Access to traditional medicines is becoming increasingly important as more and more First Nations people reclaim our culture and traditions and learn of their benefits to our overall health. First Nations people do not view our medicines from a purely mainstream medical model; rather, we understand that our plant-based medicines not only help us to fight physical health problems, but they also help us to connect to the Creator and purify, protect, and heal ourselves emotionally, mentally, and spiritually. Some of the medicines that we use in ceremony or prayer include sage, sweetgrass, tobacco, and cedar; others are not shared publicly. The use of these medicines helps to cleanse us, heal us, and take our prayers to the Creator. Medicines used to prevent or heal illness are found all around us in our traditional territories and beyond. In these times when First Nations people's health is greatly threatened by diabetes, cancer, and heart disease, we need to return to our ancestors' teachings to help return us back to our former healthy ways.

Each territory has its own indigenous plants that were used by our ancestors, and sometimes traded with people from nearby territories. As more of us learn about and accept the value of our traditional medicines, we must also have those who will become the knowledge carriers to ensure that these teachings are passed on to future generations. Who has this knowledge now in our individual communities? Who are they training? Are the medicines still grown in our territories; if not, how do we reintroduce them? Are people aware of the traditional medicines from their communities? We cannot assume that there are already identified people who will take on these important roles in the same way it used to happen generations ago. Only in rare circumstances are individuals being trained from an early age to take on specific roles in the community, so we no longer have the luxury to assume that someone else is doing it. We must ask how we can help to ensure this and many other important things are being taken care of and preserved for the seven generations to come. Some First Nations health providers are working toward incorporating traditional plants into their medical practice. A public account of such a journey is documented in a television series about Dr. Daniel Behn who travelled around the world in Vision TV's Medicine Woman series to learn about traditional medicines used by various Indigenous cultures.

The Top Five Ways Health Providers Can Help Reintroduce and Preserve First Nations Medicines

1. Learn about and adhere to the protocols of working with First Nations healers, herbalists, and Elders
2. Train those who work with First Nations people about traditional medicines, their benefits, and how to incorporate them into someone's healing plan
3. Fund the development of resources such as books, pamphlets, and videos
4. Fund the development of knowledge and reintroduction of traditional medicines into individual communities
5. Ensure equal access to traditional medicines and resources to those living off-reserve and in urban settings

Find Out More

First Nations Traditional Models of Wellness: Traditional Medicines and Practices. First Nations Health Society. 2010.
Medicine Woman TV Series. Vision TV. 2007.
Native American Ethnobotany Database. University of Michigan.
Native Plants for the Playground and their Traditional Uses. Sheila Grieve. 2010.
Plants on the Medicine Trail. Bear River First Nation Heritage and Cultural Centre.

Sidebar – Moon Time

First Nations people view a woman's Moon Time (menstruation) as a medicine unto itself. Many people believe that women who are on their Moon Time must be kept away from other medicines, ceremonies, or other sacred things. The teachings that I received say that this is necessary as Moon Time is a medicine that gives life and is too powerful to be around other medicines as it may interfere with the other medicine's powers. Those with patriarchal and foreign beliefs view Moon Time in a much less respectful way. Our ancestors believed something more spiritual and inclusive as First Nations were respectful of nature, knew that each and every thing had meaning and a significant place in the world, and were respectful of each person's gifts rather than judging or shaming them. For instance, in many communities, women would spend their Moon Time by themselves or with other women on their Moon Time in a secluded place while others brought them food, helped them in other ways, or participated in Moon Time ceremonies. This helpful behavior shows how important and sacred Moon Time was to our ancestors, and should be to us.

Food Access

Many First Nations people deal with the daily challenge of having access to enough food to eat even one meal a day, much less healthy food that would help them to achieve and maintain good health. Barriers to accessing healthy food are mainly financially based; most First Nations people live in poverty, and those in remote communities that are able to import fresh fruit and vegetables pay many times what they would have to pay in the city. Access to healthy food is being addressed in various ways in both urban and rural areas. New things that are beginning to take hold are nutrition programs, school-based food programs, access to traditional foods, agri-food conferences, traditional food guides, community kitchens, and community food fishing. On a very small scale some communities and organizations are teaching people to shop and cook on a limited budget, eat healthier, and create community gardens to show people how to grow, preserve, and cook healthy food. More prevalent efforts to stop hunger include organizations providing free or low cost food in their programs and individuals utilizing food banks. Other broad efforts by First Nations political organizations and individual communities are to change systemic issues including poverty reduction, increasing education and employment attainment, and restoring inherent hunting, fishing and gathering rights.

Programs that are helping individuals to have more access to healthy and affordable food are all important ways for us all to tackle hunger without having to wait for program funding or the new health guide to show up. What would truly help us is for more people to become involved in individual community initiatives as volunteers, funders, and supporters. We need our Elders, leaders, and other role models to become involved so that others will become encouraged to eat and live healthier. A program or initiative is only as good as the people who attend. Access to food in our traditional territories is part of the answer to this large problem. As some of our communities regain our inherent right to fish, hunt, and gather food, some people are returning to these ways, but not nearly enough. Talk show hosts and authors alike are encouraging everyone to eat more salmon, berries, and natural products – just like our traditional diet. More of us are beginning to ask very important questions of our leadership and ourselves: What are community leaders doing to help change this? Why are people not creating food gardens in our territories? Why aren't young people being trained to hunt, fish, and cook healthy meals for themselves? Who knows how to can vegetables and fruit? Why aren't Chiefs, Elders, community leaders, and other role models setting a good example by changing their lifestyles? We need more than just medical interventions; we need to change our lives.

Every year I am inspired by an Elder and her son who come to town to set up a table at the local craft fair. In fact, the main reason I go there is to buy fish that I can't fish for or preserve myself. Their table is full of canned fruit, fish sandwiches, and dried, canned and smoked fish. I am sure that is also the type of food they eat at home, but they come down to trade just like their ancestors did. The only difference is today it is for money so that they can survive in this world that they are living in. I am fortunate enough to be one of the few First Nations people who can afford to buy from them; that is my access to traditional foods.

There are also great efforts across the country that are making a real difference in how our young people are thinking about food and the land. The Urban Native Youth Association in Vancouver is focusing on educating youth with health booklets and posters, a cookbook, teaching youth to cook healthy food on a budget through hands on teaching, including only healthy foods in hampers they give to youth during the holiday season, and starting a community garden. The Muskoday Organic Growers Co-op in Saskatchewan trained 11 families in the knowledge and practice of Indigenous organic gardening over a one-year period; the food that they grew was shared with Elders and a school lunch program. Our Traditions, Our Future is a four-year educational, hands-on training project on the Alderville Reserve that will benefit 300 through teaching traditional wild rice management skills and harvesting, knowledge of wild food, and other traditional hunting and gathering practices. Students at the Nay Ah Shing Schools in Minnesota are growing vegetables that will be used in their lunches and nutrition classes; they are helped by three to ten year-olds from the Band's daycare, school staff, community members, and businesses. The Aboriginal Agricultural Education Society of British Columbia is working with the provincial government to support First Nations community gardening initiatives through the First Nations Community Food Systems for Healthy Living project. These stories need to be shared more widely so that others can join this amazing movement that will greatly enhance our lives and move us closer to the ways of our ancestors.

Find Out More

B.C. First Nation Community Nutrition Needs and Assets Survey. First Nations Health Council. 2009.
Eating Healthy On A Budget: Mind, Body & Spirit. 2nd Edition. Urban Native Youth Association. 2009.
Indigenous Plant Diva (documentary). Kamala Todd. 2008.

Addictions Treatment

As more First Nations people begin to understand that alcohol and drugs are often used as a coping mechanism to deal with low self-esteem, trauma, abandonment, anger, and many other issues, more are seeking help to overcome their addictions. Many First Nations people are living alcohol and drug free today. At least 90% of the people I know who no longer use alcohol and drugs attribute that change to understanding historical issues that have negatively affected the First Nations community and gaining a better sense of self-esteem and belonging through reconnecting to their culture and traditions. I, and many others, call this 'culture as therapy'. Many First Nations programs and alcohol and drug counsellor training programs include cultural traditions and practices such as smudging, talking circles, prayer, talking with Elders, and cultural activities to ensure that counsellors are healthy and able to fully support First Nations people on their road to recovery. Both culture and clinical therapy are being used to help address the areas that inhibit a person from feeling good about themselves, being able to handle stress, being able to seek help, or believing that they deserve a better and healthier life, all of which are key to helping individuals to shed their dependency on alcohol and drugs.

Some First Nations programs are going beyond a strictly alcohol and drug model; they are being innovative in how they work with youth to prevent and intervene in alcohol and drug use before it becomes a bigger problem. Leading Thunderbird Lodge at Fort San in the Qu'Appelle Valley, Saskatchewan is a youth addiction treatment centre which focuses on the medicine wheel to build upon strengths and a system that youth can easily follow upon exiting the program. The Manitoba Theatre for Young People's Aboriginal Program in Winnipeg offers free acting, performing and film training classes to First Nations teens. Vancouver's Urban Native Youth Association helps prevent substance abuse by working with First Nations students throughout the year and by hosting a spring break basketball camp and summer camps that help youth to develop life skills through group interactions, cultural activities, workshops, and interactions with positive role models. The National Native Alcohol and Drug Abuse Program has a network of 52 on-reserve residential treatment centres with over 700 beds for youth, families, and adults; most of these programs are operated by a First Nations community. Urban First Nations people are accessing various services at Friendship Centres, First Nations not-for-profit organizations, and non-First Nations programs.

The training of alcohol and drug counsellors is also evolving to incorporate a more integrated model of clinical practice and cultural teachings to better meet the needs of First Nations people. The Nechi Training, Research and Health Promotions Institute in Alberta is one example of such a program. Nechi incorporates both academic curriculum and First Nations traditions to train addictions counsellors. Their unique approach includes learning about gambling as an addiction and solvent abuse, students living on-site, experiential learning, and participation in traditional First Nations practices and ceremonies. Their intensive experiential training is helping to equip students with the tools they will need to help the individuals they work with and to ensure they are staying healthy and grounded while doing this stressful yet rewarding work.

Find Out More

Nechi Training, Research and Health Promotions Institute
National Native Alcohol and Drug Abuse Program Network of Treatment Centres
Manitoba Theatre for Young People's Aboriginal Program
Tsow-Tun Le Lum Substance Abuse Treatment Centre
In the Realm of Hungry Ghosts: Close Encounters With Addiction. Dr. Gabor Maté. 2009.
Addictive Behaviours Among Aboriginal People in Canada. Deborah Chansonneuve. Aboriginal Healing Foundation. 2007.
Urban Native Youth Association Alcohol & Drug Programs
Kinoondidaa'gamig Treatment Home

Humor

First Nations people are known for our humor. Without it we could not have survived the atrocities that have been put upon us. Our humor is like that of other cultural groups which includes teasing each other about our community, looks, or habits. While we might do this amongst ourselves, we certainly do not appreciate non-First Nations people doing it as they often do it in a disrespectful or demeaning way rather than an accepted way amongst those with a shared history. They have not lived our realities, so they have no idea that it is not always the joke that we are laughing at. Often it is the gross irony that is behind it that brings us to laughter.

Many say that you should not be worried if you are being teased by a First Nations person because that is when you know that they like you. If they didn't like you, they wouldn't waste their time. I am constantly surprised when in a restaurant that most often it is only our table of First Nations people who are talking, having fun, and laughing. Perhaps it is easier for us as it is our social nature that comes from a history of living communally and our oral history which taught us to interact with others as a natural way of being. I don't know for sure what makes us this way, but I am thankful.

There are a growing number of comedians, playwrights, and actors addressing the day-to-day lives of First Nations people's reality. It is great to hear and see our reality on stage in ways that we haven't before. Any form of healthy communication that helps us bring our issues to the forefront is okay with me as it helps us to begin discussions that we might not otherwise have. This is especially true with non-First Nations people so that they can understand our reality. It is quite the experience to be at a movie or live performance where something is said about First Nations people and First Nations people in the audience are the only ones laughing. I think this is partly due to it being an inside joke, but it also indicates a lack of knowledge among viewers. Movies such as Smoke Signals are meant to educate people about our lives and to start discussions, so I encourage non-First Nations to take the opportunity to ask respectful questions so that you can learn more.

RezX's Chris Tyrone Ross recently commented on the benefits of First Nations humor, but also noted the pitfalls of helping to stereotype ourselves through our humor. Comedians are not responsible for ensuring their audience understands that they are exaggerating or being sarcastic, but they must know that some are likely to believe the stereotype, so I think they have a responsibility to tread carefully so as not to add to the problem. Some First Nations comedians to watch out for include Don Kelly, Ryan McMahon, Cliff Paul, Skeena Reece, Monique Hurteau, Don Burnstick, and Darrell Dennis.

Find Out More

Me Funny. Compiled and edited by Drew Haydon Taylor. Douglas & McIntyre. 2005.
Jesters of the Rez. First Story. CTV. 2010.
Gatherings - Volume VIII Shaking the Belly: Releasing the Sacred Clown. Theytus Books. 1997.

Parenting

Reintroducing healthy parenting skills into our families is one of the best ways for First Nations to reverse many of the negative effects of residential schools in our communities. If our families are offered culturally appropriate parenting skills that are based on teaching skills and building on strengths rather than blame and·shame, there can be significant change in one generation in our communities. I have seen this play out in my own life. When my children were young, it was a struggle to learn to be a parent, to show affection, to say 'I love you' once they were no longer babies, to speak only words of encouragement, and many other things that should be much easier for anyone in this day and age. Without many positive role models and an awareness that I had to push myself to get past my blocks, I would never have become a better parent that was open, loving, and supportive of my children.

There are many small parenting programs across the country, but not nearly enough. Those programs that are accessible to our families are making significant change, one family at a time. The most effective programs or workshops are based on traditional First Nations parenting practices, focus on people's strengths, and teach positive communication, cultural learning, and lifeskills development. The most effective programs involve both the caregivers and the children such as the Strengthening Families Program which focuses on reducing the risk of family breakdown by helping to increase family communication, bonding, strengths and resilience. The Urban Native Youth Association recently produced a youth-friendly parenting booklet that focuses on Belonging, Activity, Learning, Acknowledgment, Nurturing, Compassion, and Engagement (BALANCE) to help youth to become the parent they wish they had. Mainstream programs that have been successful in becoming more culturally appropriate include Nobody's Perfect and Head Start.

Find Out More

Nobody's Perfect Parenting Program

First Nations Parents Club in First Nations Schools Association

BALANCE: Parenting Booklet for Native Youth. Urban Native Youth Association. 2011.

Education

First Nations graduation rates from secondary and post-secondary schools are increasing in many communities due primarily to the concerted efforts of First Nations people fighting for the development of culturally appropriate programs and First Nations run schools, the inclusion of First Nations history in school curriculum and books, the hiring of knowledgeable First Nations staff, and other equally important actions. Those First Nations youth who are doing better in school are often attending on-reserve First Nations run schools, one of the few First Nations post-secondary schools in urban settings, or an alternative program that is culturally appropriate, welcoming, and relevant to First Nations people. Of course, some First Nations youth are doing just fine in mainstream schools, but not nearly enough to even say that is a good option for all of our youth at this time.

Schools that are making a concerted effort to engage, support, and welcome First Nations students are having the most success. Some unique efforts include: 1) The Amiskwaciy Academy in Edmonton which is open to any student who is interested in learning while embracing First Nations culture and history through both indoor and outdoor learning experiences in areas such as science, history, and social studies; 2) Wisconsin Tribes who have created everything from curriculum resources to a turtle shaped school that is operated from a traditional clan system and teachings; 3) The First Nations University of Canada which has campuses in Saskatchewan and offers undergraduate and graduate degrees within an environment of First Nations history and culture; 4) The Native Education College in Vancouver offers a culturally appropriate educational environment that includes a family violence resource library, employment readiness training, adult basic education, and college transfer courses; 5) The Seventh Generation Club encourages First Nations students to make healthy choices, stay in school, and participate in school and community activities; 6) First Nations SchoolNet provides internet connectivity and computer hardware assistance to First Nations schools; and 7) Eel Ground School near Miramichi New Brunswick was named one of Canada's most technologically advanced schools.

There is no longer any excuse for the failure to educate First Nations children. There are many sources of information, curriculum, training, partnerships, and other things that can help mainstream schools better serve First Nations people. Information can be found online, in research reports, in libraries, and directly from the First Nations community groups that are working tirelessly to help our children have a positive experience in school. Here are what I think are 10 easy ways to help First Nations students do well both academically and socially in school:

1. Include the true history of North America from first contact to modern times in the curriculum
2. Include the true history and strengths of First Nations people within the curriculum
3. Make the school and classroom a welcoming place for First Nations parents and include them in activities other than just teaching beading or making bannock
4. Remember that most First Nations people live in poverty, so decrease or waive fees for outings, lunches, and extra curricular activities to ensure that First Nations youth have equal access to these important things that help to increase their chance of staying in, and doing well in school
5. Ensure issues of racism and bullying are addressed immediately and at a systemic level
6. Ensure that First Nations youth have equal access to homework clubs and tutors
7. Ensure that First Nations parents have equal access to programs that teach parents how to help their child study and learn
8. Continue evaluating what schools and schools districts are doing and seek out best practices to implement
9. In urban settings, partner with First Nations and other not-

for-profit organizations to help provide supports to First Nations children, youth, and families

10. Hire qualified First Nations teachers and administrators, or if they aren't available, then hire and train others who are committed to helping First Nations students to succeed

Find Out More

Seventh Generation Club
National Indian Education Association
First Nations Education Steering Committee
First Nations University of Canada
Winds of Change Magazine. AISES Publishing, Inc. for the American Indian Science & Engineering Society.
Children of the Earth High School in Winnipeg Manitoba
The State of Aboriginal Learning in Canada: A Holistic Approach to Measuring Success. Canadian Council on Learning. 2009.
Protecting Indigenous Knowledge and Heritage: A Global Challenge. Marie Battiste and James (Sákéj) Youngblood Henderson. 2000.
National Indian Education Association (USA)

Early Childhood Development

More and more First Nations people are relearning the importance of providing cultural, social, and educational supports to our children before they enter elementary school. I say 'relearn', as our communities were based upon continual teaching and learning throughout a person's life, so it is not something new to us. Today, communities are developing culturally appropriate early childhood development (ECD) programs that include culture, parental involvement, Elders, and basic learning skills. These programs are better preparing our children to do well both academically and socially in elementary school. They are also engaging parents to become more involved in and supportive of their child's learning experiences. Aboriginal Head Start Programs have seen great success with First Nations children and families as they include cultural learning opportunities for children and their caregivers. Successful initiatives such as the Katl'odeeche First Nation Children's Centre on the Hay River Dene Reserve in the Northwest Territories incorporate culture by teaching language, creating crafts, singing traditional songs, and learning about ceremonies; the Aboriginal HIPPY Program helps parents to prepare their children to enter kindergarten; and the BC Aboriginal Childcare Society loans early childhood education curriculum boxes to First Nations childcare programs to ensure First Nations children have access to First Nations focused books and other learning materials.

The First Nations Child & Family Caring Society of Canada (FNCFCSC) has made great strides in recent years in raising the profile of ECD issues within First Nations and non-First Nations communities. Their work with the United Nations, policy developers, and governments has led to very useful research that will help to build a solid foundation for ongoing support to First Nations children. Some communities are being creative with their limited space and resources by utilizing closely located programs as a hub of services that engage and involve parents in healthy activities to strengthen their parenting skills while also exposing them to other services that can be helpful to them and their children. There are more First Nations ECD and childcare programs being developed, but there needs to be many more given our young population and ever-growing numbers. Government funders must see this as a priority and essential building block for communities before there will be significant positive change in our community. The Assembly of First Nations and FNCFCSC have both issued many reports and statements that paint a clear picture for governments and funders to follow in order to better meet the needs of First Nations children.

Find Out More

Caring for First Nations Children Society
First Nations Child & Family Caring Society of Canada
First Nations Early Learning and Child Care Action Plan. Assembly of First Nations. 2005.
Handbook of Best Practices in Aboriginal Early Childhood Programs. BC Aboriginal Child Care Society. 2003.
Aboriginal Children's Circle of Early Learning
Aboriginal HIPPY (Home Instruction for Parents of Preschool Youngsters)
Aboriginal Head Start Programs

Canoe Journeys

Since time immemorial First Nations people across the continent have travelled via canoe to their hunting or fishing grounds, to trade with other communities, and many other things. By the mid-1900s most sea-going canoes were in museums or no longer being carved. In the 1980s several Northwest Coast communities carved canoes and nine canoes participated in *Paddle to Seattle* as a part of Washington State's bi-centennial celebrations. This was followed up in 1993 when 30 canoes from all along the Northwest Coast travelled to Bella Bella, B.C. Barb Cranmer documented this incredible journey in her film *Qutuwas: People Gathering Together* which takes viewers on an amazing physical, emotional, mental, and spiritual journey with paddlers. These two canoe journeys were some of the most significant in helping to revitalize the great canoeing tradition of the Northwest Coast. Now, every year there are several canoe journeys that take place on the Northwest Coast during the summer months. Some last a few days, while others are weeks long and include hundreds of miles of pulling.

One of the greatest benefits of any canoe journey is the experiential learning that participants are exposed to. Most journeys include visiting First Nations communities along the route where the canoes and pullers are welcomed ashore in a traditional ceremony that involves the protocols used by our ancestors. Paddlers participate in a community celebration in the evening that includes many aspects of culture including songs, dances, welcoming ceremonies, prayer, gift giving, and blessing. Many participants, especially from the urban setting, may not have grown up amongst these traditions, so they learn a tremendous amount during the journey. For these individuals, the journey is especially significant, and often life changing. Most speak of the strong sense of self that they gain, as well as a sense of belonging, pride, and history. Their participation shows them that a different life is possible and that their First Nations heritage is something to be proud of. The Tlicho Government in the Northwest Territories hosts canoe trips for youth to paddle to the Tåîchô Annual Gathering as a way to help youth learn about the land, traditions, and canoeing traditions of their ancestors.

More and more urban organizations are participating in canoe journeys every year to help ensure that youth are exposed to these important experiences that can help them gain a better understanding of themselves as First Nations individuals. Most times it is not in a traditionally hand-made canoe, but it is a canoe all the same. In B.C., the RCMP has partnered with First Nations people to host the annual *Pulling Together Canoe Journey* that helps to build bridges between the two groups.

Find Out More

Northwest Native Canoe Centre in Seattle, Washington.
Qutuwas: People Gathering Together, Barb Cranmer. 1997.
Tribal Journeys Website

Sports

There are a number of sports to which First Nations people have made significant contributions, including Canada's national summer sport of lacrosse, hockey, kayaking, and arctic games. Many do not know that First Nations people created the game of lacrosse. Lacrosse would sometimes include hundreds of players and would go on for days at a time. It was used as a way to train for war as well as sport. There is some speculation that hockey started in a First Nations community, but hockey historians claim that it has been around in some similar form around the world for thousands of years. Snowshoes have been used around the world for various amounts of time. First Nations people were using many different forms of snowshoes when the first Europeans arrived on our shores. While canoes can be found through history in various places around the world, none are as large as the sea-going cedar canoes of First Nations communities that could hold over 50 people and navigate the open waters of the ocean. The kayak was created by the Inuit of Canada's north. These are just a few of the ways in which First Nations people have contributed to sport, so keep your eyes and ears open for more.

Most First Nations children and youth will be found participating in activities such as soccer, basketball, or other sports that are free, affordable, or one of the few that are played in their remote community. Since many popular sports such as hockey, tennis, football, or martial arts are expensive to play and to buy the equipment needed, many First Nations cannot participate as most of us live in poverty. Initiatives that are helping to identify, encourage, support, and sponsor First Nations athletes range from pick-up baseball teams, to talent identification camps, to what is viewed as the First Nations Olympics – the North American Indigenous Games. Some of the larger or more concentrated (although under-funded) efforts to promote sport and fitness amongst First Nations people include: the Aboriginal Sport Circle, which is the national coordinating body for First Nations' recognition of sports excellence and athletes, coaching, and community development initiatives; the North American Indigenous Games, which drew over 7,000 athletes in 2009 includes cultural activities, concerts, and arts and crafts vendors; the Arctic Winter Games is a multi-cultural event that includes Dene and Inuit games such as one-foot high kick, knuckle hop, dog mushing, snowshoeing, and other more mainstream sports; the Native American Sports Council promotes athletic excellence and wellness through sports programs which combine traditional values with those of the modern Olympics, with the additional goal of enabling emerging elite athletes to be identified and developed for national, international and Olympic competition; Promoting Life-skills for Aboriginal Youth (P.L.A.Y.) is a pilot project being developed by Right To Play in partnership with the Moose Cree First Nation in Ontario; and Nike N7, which expanded to Canada from the U.S. in 2010, is intended to encourage youth who are not active in sport to become involved, to promote leadership, and to use sport as a springboard to other healthy activities.

Sports teams using First Nations names for their name and associated logos and cartoonish characters as mascots helps to perpetuate negative stereotypes about First Nations people. This can be witnessed in the National Football League, Major League Baseball, and at universities, colleges, and high schools. Some teams have jerseys with First Nations people depicted as cartoonish characters; other teams encourage their fans to do the tomahawk chop or ridiculous 'war dances'; and some even chant a stereotypical Hollywood version of what they think is a First Nations song, with many young impressionable people receiving the message that it is okay to do so. In order to stop the negative stereotyping of First Nations people, there have been a few significant actions taken by First Nations and non-First Nations people alike. The National Coalition on Racism in Sports and Media has called for the elimination of the use of First Nations people and cultural symbols from sport for years and many artists have drawn caricatures of other ethnic groups to show how offended they might be if it was their people who were being stereotyped and insulted in the public eye.

There are some well accomplished First Nations athletes in various sports; here are just a few:

Olympians – Waneek Horn-Miller in water polo; Colette Bourgojne won 10 medals in both the paralympic winter games in sit-skiing and summer games in wheelchair racing from 1992-2010; Alwyn Morris won bronze and gold in canoeing; Richard Peter won two golds in wheelchair basketball; Billy Mills won gold in the 10,000 meters; and Jim Thorpe won gold medals in both the decathlon and the pentathlon at the 1912 Stockholm Olympics. In 1950, the United States press selected Jim Thorpe as the most outstanding athlete of the first half of the 20th Century, and he was awarded ABC's Wide World of Sports' Athlete of the Century.

National Hockey League – Jonathan Cheechoo, Gino Odjick, Jordan Tootoo, Sandy McCarthy, Carey Price, Denny Lambert, Chris Simon, Reggie Leach, Bryan Trottier, Stan Jonathan, Ron Delorme (also NHL scout), and Ted Nolan who also went on to win the NHL Coach of the Year Award.

Lacrosse – Both the women's and men's Iroquois Teams compete in international competitions essentially as their own country

Find Out More

Chiefs and Champions on APTN Television
Tears and Triumphs on APTN Television
Great Athletes from Our First Nations. Vincent Schilling. Second Story Press. 2007.
National Coalition on Racism in Sport and the Media.
Jim Thorpe Original All-American. Joseph Bruchac. Dial Books. 2006.
Aboriginal Sport Circle
North American Indigenous Games
Arctic Winter Games

National Aboriginal Day & National Aboriginal History Month

National Aboriginal Day (NAD) was declared a national day of celebration in 1996 due to the ongoing lobbying efforts that First Nations people had taken since 1982. Many people are disappointed that it is not a national holiday, especially since it is a day to celebrate the First Nations of Canada. If there is a Canada Day, Labour Day, and Boxing Day, then National Aboriginal Day surely should be important enough to be declared a national holiday. June 21 was chosen as National Aboriginal Day because of the cultural significance of the summer solstice - it is the first day of summer and longest day of the year. Setting aside a day for First Nations people is part of the wider recognition of First Nations' important place within the fabric of Canada and their ongoing contributions as First Peoples. In 2009, this effort was expanded by the Parliament of Canada which unanimously declared June as National Aboriginal History Month.

Despite only having access to limited funds, communities across the land are utilizing NAD as a means to come together to celebrate First Nations culture and existence with mainstream Canada and to share our history and culture with non-First Nations people. Most events are open to the public, and many are free. Each event varies in what they offer – food, art, crafts, clothing, videos, speakers, sports, talent competitions, tipis, and diverse performers in the areas of hip hop, jazz, traditional dance groups, rock, throat singing, and spoken word. So come out and join us in celebrating First Nations culture, history, and traditions.

Sadly, in many cities and towns there is still barely a mention of NAD in the media, especially before it happens, despite being alerted by organizers. Some television channels and newspapers mention NAD after it happens, so many people don't even know about the events until they are over. Media coverage is nowhere near what Chinese New Year, Diwali, or the Santa Claus parade receives. This purposeful neglect is likely representative of what many non-First Nations people in the media think of NAD – that no one cares. This is likely due primarily to the lack of awareness of the day and the fact that it is not a national holiday. I believe that if there was more acknowledgement of the day, more positive stories about First Nations people, and better advertising, that many non-First Nations people would come and join us in our celebrations.

A Brief History of National Aboriginal Day

- 1982 – National Indian Brotherhood (now the Assembly of First Nations) calls for the creation of June 21 as National Aboriginal Solidarity Day

- 1995 – Royal Commission on Aboriginal Peoples recommends the designation of a National First Peoples Day. The Sacred Assembly, a national conference of Aboriginal and non-Aboriginal people chaired by Elijah Harper, calls for a national holiday to celebrate the contributions of Aboriginal peoples.

- June 13, 1996 – Former Governor General Roméo LeBlanc declares June 21 as National Aboriginal Day

- June 2009 – After two years of pressure by the New Democratic Party, the Parliament of Canada votes unanimously to declare June as National Aboriginal History Month

How to Find a National Aboriginal Day Event Near You

Most events are not reported in the news before they happen, so you need to seek out information which is usually posted as flyers, in newsletters, or on websites. Here are a few sources:

- Municipal websites may list some events in their city

- Aboriginal Day Live. Aboriginal People's Television

Network (APTN)

- Friendship Centres often host events or know where they are being held
- Most First Nations organizations will know what is happening in their community as they are often the ones organizing them
- Indian & Northern Affairs Canada website lists events from across the country

Language Preservation

Language is the basis of culture. It evolves to meet a people's needs in relation to their environment, belief system, and interactions with others. The Inuit for example have numerous words for snow as they realize the significance of different types of snow and how it impacts their daily lives in relation to their ability to hunt, gather, travel, or simply exist. Most First Nations languages have words that have significant meaning in relation to the Creator, greetings, honoring, positions of responsibility, and other things that cannot be translated into English without losing its true meaning and significance. In addition, our interactions with others are governed by protocols that are reflected in our languages and hold great meaning. These are but a few of the significant reasons why preserving First Nations language is incredibly important.

There are over 50 First Nations languages within 11 language families in Canada, with over 60% of those being in British Columbia. This density of languages in a single region is only outnumbered by Oklahoma which has many language groups due to the forced relocation of many Nations to that area as America was expanding westward. Only three First Nations languages in Canada – Inuktitut, Cree, and Ojibway – are considered to be safe from extinction; most others are in danger of becoming extinct, and many are extinct. Some Nations have as few as two fluent speakers remaining. Because of this grim reality, there is a mad rush across North America by First Nations people to preserve First Nations languages by training new speakers, videotaping and audio recording speakers, and documenting as much of their language as possible. We no longer have time to ignore this issue – to not audio or video record them now will definitely lead to the loss of languages, and only writing down the language would mean losing the nuances of speaking the language forever.

Even though governments brought this reality upon First Nations people by implementing policies and laws that led to forbidding our children to speak their traditional language, they are not making meaningful funding contributions to ensure our languages are preserved and that new speakers are trained. The funding that is put towards language preservation is a miniscule effort to save an incredibly important part of our culture. Governments understood the importance of our languages in maintaining and transmitting cultural knowledge, which is why they made a huge effort to try to kill our languages off. There is no good reason not to help revitalize it now. Governments paid teachers across the country to stop us from speaking our languages in residential schools through shaming, threats, and physical punishment including having pins stuck through children's tongues, so governments should be paying teachers now to help us relearn our languages.

Despite the overall lack of funding, resources, and support, there are various efforts across North America to save First Nations languages. Efforts include documenting language and speakers via video, audio, and print; teaching language in First Nations schools when and if there are speakers and funds to teach the children; the development of online language dictionaries, conferences, language immersion camps, and even a few Ipod apps. While these efforts seem very hopeful, they are happening at such a small scale and such a late time that it may not be enough. Many more resources are needed from governments and the private sector to help provide funding, recording equipment, technical assistance, and many other things if there is to be a real chance at saving the remaining languages.

Find Out More

First Peoples' Heritage, Language and Culture Council
Culture Camps for Language Learning: An Immersion Handbook. First Peoples' Heritage, Language and Culture Council. 2010.
Report on the Status of B.C. First Nations Languages 2010. First Peoples' Heritage, Language and Culture Council. 2010.

Native American Language Immersion: Innovative Native Education for Children & Families. Janine Pease-Pretty On Top.
Native Youth & Culture Fund. First Nations Development Institute.
Language and Culture as Protective Factors for At-Risk Communities. Onowa McIvor, Art Napoleon and M. Dickie. Journal of Aboriginal Health. 2009.
From Generation to Generation: Survival and Maintenance of Canada's Aboriginal Languages within Families, Communities and Cities map. Indian and Northern Affairs Canada. 2002.

Child Welfare – Returning Responsibility

Across the country, First Nations child welfare agencies are either operating or in development in both on-reserve and urban settings. At the centre of this positive change must be the recognition that First Nations people have the inherent right, will, knowledge, and commitment to create a new system that will better serve the long-term needs of First Nations communities and our children. Each agency is somewhere along the continuum from community consultations to full-fledged delegated authority which includes being bound by provincial child welfare legislation. There is great hope that providing culturally appropriate services to our own people will lead to children staying safely in their own home by helping to stem the tide of child apprehensions and family breakdown. However, the First Nations community is painfully aware that many other issues continue to lead to the separation of our children from their family, community, and culture, including social and economic issues that must also be addressed if there is to be meaningful and lasting change. One of the main challenges for these agencies is to assure First Nations people that they will not simply be brown faces perpetuating a system that has historically not worked.

While the transfer of services to the First Nations communities is very exciting and creates great hope, there are still many challenges that must be addressed before these agencies can really begin to help families make changes in their lives to better support their children and themselves. The First Nations Child & Family Caring Society of Canada (FNCFCSC) has brought national attention to the fact that on-reserve First Nations agencies receive only 72% in funding in comparison to what non-First Nations agencies do. This ultimately leads to less opportunity to implement new ideas, since a large amount of funding must go towards salaries, paying foster parents, and other non-preventative services. Other issues include a lack of funding for prevention programs, the high cost and redirection of human resources to make changes that comply with ever-changing provincial legislation, a lack of First Nations and non-First Nations foster parents who can provide a welcoming, nurturing, and safe environment for First Nations children, and a shortage of qualified First Nations social workers to carry out this important work. So while First Nations agencies have the will and expertise to create a system that will better serve the needs of First Nations children and families, their progress is being limited by funding and other relevant issues.

The most effective child welfare programs work to prevent children from being apprehended in the first place, reunite families as soon as possible, train foster parents to be welcoming, nurturing, and safe places for First Nations children to live, include cultural traditions and practices, and are supportive rather than punitive of parents who are struggling. Although First Nations agencies are working with fewer resources than non-First Nations agencies, they are doing their best to make significant changes while ensuring that they are keeping children safe. They consult with Elders and cultural teachers to help ensure that they are introducing culture into their practice as much as possible and are providing opportunities for children to remain connected to their family and First Nations community. A few of the many successful agencies include the Yellowhead Tribal Services Agency in Alberta which is integrating customary adoption practices with provincial adoption laws; the Vancouver Aboriginal Child and Family Services Society helps teach parenting and communications skills through its Strengthening Families Program to try to help create a network of support for the children before or after they are in foster care, and brings children in foster care to visit their First Nations communities; the Native Child and Family Services of Toronto offers a wide range of programming for all ages to help develop cultural and life skills and strengthen relationships; and the National Youth in Care Network provides opportunities for youth to share valuable input to improve child welfare services. These are the types of innovative things that must happen in order to greatly reduce the number of First Nations children being taken into the custody of the provinces.

Find Out More

Reconciliation in Child Welfare: Touchstones of Hope for Indigenous Children, Youth, and Families. Cindy Blackstock, et al. First Nations Child & Family Caring Society. 2005.
Wen: De. We Are Coming to the Light of Day. First Nations Child & Family Caring Society of Canada. 2005.
Aboriginal and Practice Standards and Indicators. Caring for First Nations Children Society. 2005.
Aski Awasis/Children of the Earth: First Peoples Speaking on Adoption. Ed., Jeanine Carriere. Fernwood Publishing. 2010.
Aboriginal Children and Youth in Canada: Canada Must Do Better. Canadian Council of Provincial Child and Youth Advocates. 2010.

Spotlight – The First Nations Child & Family Caring Society of Canada has been at the forefront in educating Canadian and international audiences about the day-to-day reality for First Nations children and has developed many innovative ways for everyone to be a part of the solution that will keep First Nations children safe. Their initiatives include the *First People's Child & Family Review Journal*, strategic research partnerships, Caring Across Boundaries photo exhibit, and curriculum based on their *Touchstones of Hope* Report for Bachelors and Masters of Social Work programs. FNCFCSC promotes seven free ways for the average person to make a difference, including Be A Witness, Sign Jordan's Principle, Support Shannen's Dream, Sign the Touchstones of Hope, Engage Young People, Many Hands One Dream, and Make a Donation to help ensure they are able to continue to be at the forefront in changing child welfare practice so that the systems are adapting to better meet the needs of First Nations children and their families.

Volunteerism

Volunteerism in the First Nations community is not a well understood area. Many people assume that because we do not have lots of formal volunteer programs or registered volunteers, that we don't utilize or have many volunteers in our community. The truth is that we usually do not name voluntary work as volunteerism; we usually just jump in to help get things done. When an event is happening we simply say 'we need someone to help with….', not 'we need a volunteer.' So while there is not usually any formal naming of it, volunteerism is alive and well in First Nations communities. In fact, our communities could not function without volunteers. We require volunteers to help with our community activities, host fundraising events, cook at our feasts, host visitors, serve on committees, look after children while others help at events, keep on-reserve fire stations functioning, coach sports teams, work in schools, and many other important community activities. Volunteerism in First Nations communities is a normal part of everyday life, it's not something we usually do to fill in our spare time, as a way to keep busy in our retirement years, or because we need it to build up our resume; rather, we do it because we know it is important to help out in our community. Of course, we get the same personal satisfaction that other volunteers do, but it's couched in a different way.

First Nations communities and organizations could greatly benefit from the help of volunteers, and volunteering is starting to become more formalized in First Nations not-for-profit organizations. It would be great if more non-First Nations people volunteered for First Nations' organizations. Of course it is easier to do that in an urban setting than on-reserve. However, there are reserves that are close to cities and towns that would welcome volunteers either in person or those who can help from a long distance through the wonders of the internet and email. Urban First Nations organizations are welcoming all volunteers as we can use all the help we can get to complete the important work that needs to be done. We want to help train those who will be working in our community, and it is a great way to facilitate cross-cultural learning. Best of all would be the establishment of local, provincial, and national First Nations volunteer organizations that can promote volunteerism amongst First Nations and non-First Nations people within urban, rural, and on-reserve First Nations communities and organizations.

Find Out More

Annotated Bibliography on the Nature and Extent of Collaboration Between the Voluntary Sector and First Nations Child and Family Service Agencies in Canada. S. Nadjiwan and C. Blackstock. First Nations Child and Family Caring Society of Canada. 2003.

Chapter 6

Arts

Today's First Nations artists are our contemporary storytellers. They are at the forefront of revitalizing First Nations culture, traditions, and communities by sharing our individual and collective history, hopes, dreams, and realities with the world. Their inspiring work is reaching diverse people in many forms including video, print, audio, internet, and many other mediums that allow them to express themselves and raise their voice through their own creativity. Whether traditional, contemporary, or a fusion of the two, First Nations artists are paving the way by inspiring others to pursue their own dreams, express themselves, and educate others about First Nations people.

Artists are inherently storytellers; they utilize the arts to express themselves and convey something to others whether it be emotional, mental, spiritual, or intellectual. While our ancestors passed on knowledge and history through stories, pictographs, songs, dances, and ceremonies, today's First Nations storytellers utilize both traditional and contemporary means to convey their message. Our writers, videographers, film makers, artists, musicians, actors, and singers are leading the way in reclaiming our voice as First Nations people.

Music

First Nations music is very diverse. Our singers, song writers, producers, and musicians are represented in traditional First Nations music, opera, hip hop, jazz, blues, country, folk, and many other mainstream music forms. To lump all music into traditional or contemporary is to understate the sheer volume of musical creativity that is emerging from individuals and communities across North America. Both contemporary and traditional music are being utilized to entertain, inspire, educate, and move us to action on issues such as climate change, protecting Indigenous cultures, being better people, racism, poverty, sexism, and creating a better world.

Traditional First Nations music can now be enjoyed on CD, the internet, and DVD. Individuals and groups share their music in concert halls, at pow-wows, and in ceremony. Plains drum groups that can be found at a pow-wow near you include Red Bull, Northern Cree, Porcupine Singers, and Silver Cloud. Artists such as Ulali, Joe Tohonnie Jr., Walela, and Meewasin Oma all utilize various traditional instruments to accompany their outstanding voices and styles. Tanya Tagaq, Sylvia Cloutier, and Celina Kalluk have introduced us to the wonderment of Inuit throat singing, and David Maracle, Mary Youngblood, and R. Carlo Nakai keep alive the meditative tones of traditional flute music. While many First Nations people are sharing their music with the world, there are other songs, instruments, and accompanying dances that are kept solely within the community to honor and respect their spiritual and ceremonial purposes.

More artists are beginning to fuse traditional and contemporary music through both sounds and words. Like our ancestors, we continue to adapt to changing times while keeping our cultures intact. Artists known for this include Sandy Scofield, Akina Shirt, Eagle and Hawk, Cris Dirksen, Jason Burnstick, Skeena Reece, and Susan Aglukark. Tanya Tagaq's fusion of traditional Inuit throat singing with full orchestras, English words, and jazz bands sends you on a journey over the arctic tundra into a history rich with connections to the land and nature. Even those who have found mainstream music success continue to return to their First Nations roots. Despite their widespread mainstream music success, Buffy Sainte-Marie, Robbie Robertson, Joanne Shenandoah, and Rita Coolidge have inspired many First Nations people by remaining true to their First Nations roots and connected to the community.

Artists known for their contemporary music include Murray Porter, Shane Yellowbird, Shakti Hayes, George Leach, Art Napoleon, Crystal Shawanda, and conductor John Kim Bell who was the first ever First Nations person to conduct a symphony orchestra. Hip hop has opened up an avenue for our young people to tell their stories, voice their angst, and challenge us to do better: Eekwol, Seventh Generation, Rapsure Risin, Inez Jasper, OS12, Feenix, and War Party are all known for their empowering tracks. It is inspiring to see youth put to lyrics that which others are uncomfortable talking about. They challenge history, ageism, social problems, and what it is we think First Nations youth should be, say, or do. First Nations hip hop may sometimes be raw, but quite often it is filled with words of hope, encouragement, and empowerment. It is focused on raising awareness about First Nations realities and making positive change. Our youth are utilizing this youth-friendly medium as a way to find their voice and speak their truth while inspiring others.

When watching the Junos, Grammies, or Aboriginal Music Awards, you can now find First Nations people in categories other than in just First Nations or world music. While a few First Nations music makers have broken into mainstream radio and concert halls, many more continue to struggle to find their way in. Amazing artists like Derek Miller have yet to gain the recognition that they deserve for their artistry. His great blues music has not been recognized at nearly the level it should be in mainstream music circles. Hopefully, his recent appearance at the closing ceremonies of the 2010 Winter Olympics will lead to more air time.

Find Out More

Buffy Sainte-Marie: A Multimedia Life (CD/DVD Set)
Cradleboard Teaching Project. The Nihewan Foundation for Native American Education.
Canadian Aboriginal Music Awards
Native American Music Awards

Spotlight – Buffy Sainte-Marie

Buffy Sainte-Marie has been paving the way for First Nations artists for four decades. I think of her as our own First Nations Tina Turner. She not only entertains; she challenges, educates, and inspires. Her song Universal Soldier was inducted into the Canadian Songwriters Hall of Fame in 2005, her songs have been recorded by Elvis Presley, Joe Cocker, Barbara Streisand, and many others, and her song Up Where We Belong won an Oscar for best song in 1983. Buffy's longevity is only surpassed by her creativity and commitment to making the world a better place through her music, mentorship, five years on Sesame Street, public speeches, digital art, philanthropy, and the Cradleboard Teaching Project. Cradleboard is an online resource for educators who want to learn more about First Nations culture and share it with their students; it also provides opportunities for children to learn about First Nations culture through an online peer network.

Literature

Writing is one of the most accessible ways for First Nations people to express themselves and to reach a broad audience. It can cost no more than a pencil and paper or access to a computer, so even the poorest of people can express themselves and potentially earn a living. From toddlers to policy is what you'll find in the First Nations' section of your local book store, although usually it is just a small shelf despite the vast array of books written by First Nations people. First Nations authors are producing diverse works, which may or may not focus on First Nations people or issues. Their diversity spans across fiction, non-fiction, humor, romance, mystery, autobiography, how-to books, children's stories, comics, history, academic, and endless more categories of work for us all to enjoy and learn from. Like any other author, we have something to say and we love it when everyone reads it, not just First Nations readers.

First Nations writers are utilizing many ways to get their words and thoughts out to the world. The most recent and far reaching expansion has been on the internet through websites, blogs, tweeting, or social networking. Publishing our thoughts and stories is not limited to books; rather we are increasingly utilizing newspapers, magazines, zines, comic books, and graphic novels. Self-publishing and e-literature are opening doors to those of us who would not otherwise consider ourselves writers or do not want to be published commercially. First Nations-run publishing houses like Theytus Books, Pemmican Publishing, and Kegedonce Press are leading the way in identifying, working with, and introducing First Nations authors to the world. Their commitment to ensuring First Nations voice, history, and creativity are recognized and celebrated is greatly enriching the field of literature that is available for the general public to enjoy. Close behind are non-First Nations publishers, including university presses that are open to all voices and are working with First Nations authors to get their creativity and stories out to the world. Some publishers only work with those who are already established, but others are also interested in identifying and promoting new authors such as myself. If the world is to discover both new and established First Nations writers, we need more publishers to support these bold voices that can greatly enrich Canadian literature.

Some of the most prolific and well-known First Nations writers include Lee Maracle, Drew Haydon Taylor, Joy Harjo, Marilyn Dumont, Chrystos, Sherman Alexie, Louise Erdrich, Tomson Highway, Thomas King, and Eden Robinson. Their work has paved the way for the rest of us to put to paper that which is important to us. Other equally important fiction and non-fiction authors include Howard Adams, Taiaiake Alfred, Dr. Joanne Archibald, Jeanette Armstrong, Joanne Arnott, Joseph Boyden, Beth Brant, Maria Campbell, Doug Cuthand, Vine Deloria Jr., Paula Gunn Allen, Rita Joe, Michael Kusugake, Winona LaDuke, Sandra Laronde, Dr. Beatrice Medicine, Patricia Monture, Gregory Scofield, John Trudell, Richard Van Camp, and Richard Wagamese. These individuals are not limited to being simply writers; they are also orators, actors, educators, mentors, and community leaders. Their work can also be found in published anthologies and collections of First Nations writing and in magazines and newspapers across North America. More and more our authors are moving away from being relegated only to the First Nations section of bookstores as publishers and the general public are embracing the idea that First Nations writers have important things to say about many issues, not just First Nations ones. There will always be a need for a First Nations section so that those interested in finding out more about First Nations people, issues, and thoughts can easily find us, but it is great to be in the fiction, humor, or history sections as well.

Find Out More

An Anthology of Canadian Native Literature in English (2005)

Gatherings I through X. Theytus Books.

Red Ink Magazine. Red Ink Publications.

Redwire Magazine

Visual Art

Visual art is an ever expanding field within the First Nations community. You will now find First Nations artists' work on t-shirts, book covers, prints, computer screens, photography, film, on stage, logos, web pages, and as public murals. We will always find our art in the form of totem poles, prints, masks, drums, rattles, and our traditional regalia, but just like other parts of culture, visual art continues to evolve to match our current reality. First Nations artists are utilizing modern techniques and spaces to express themselves. Buffy Sainte Marie uses her computer to create beautiful digital images; Jane Ash Poitras uses mixed media to open our eyes to history; Phil Gray incorporated stop-motion animation to illustrate the incredible amount of work it takes to create a single carved mask and designed an Olympic gold medalist's helmet; Louie Gong walks in two worlds with his unique painted shoes; Brian Jungen re-purposes runners to make masks; Corrine Hunt's art adorns Olympic medals and furniture; and Marianne Nicholson summoned the ancestors to join our human realm from dusk to dawn with *The House of the Ghosts* on the facade of the Vancouver Art Gallery. Their work is a tiny sampling of diverse creativity that is exploding in First Nations visual art. Things can only get more interesting and exciting from here.

One area in particular that has grown by leaps and bounds is film. You can find full length features, documentaries, and short films in the various film festivals across North America and beyond, on Youtube, and anywhere else film makers can share their work. Some of the more well-known First Nations film festivals include the imagineNATIVE Film and Media Arts Festival in Toronto, the IMAGeNation Aboriginal Film & Video Festival in Vancouver, the Manito Ahbee Festival in Winnipeg, the Cowichan International Aboriginal Festival of Film and Art in Duncan, B.C., Dreamspeakers Film Festival in Edmonton, Winnipeg's Aboriginal Film Festival, and the American Indian Film Festival in San Francisco. Theatre also continues to be an accessible medium for First Nations people to express themselves, and many new television shows are being broadcast on the Aboriginal People's Television Network and online.

Find Out More
Imaginative Film Festival
Manito Ahbee Festival
American Indian Film Festival
Challenging Traditions: Contemporary First Nations Art of the Northwest Coast. Ian M. Thom. Douglas & McIntyre. 2009.
Aboriginal People's Television Network
Inuit Women Artists. Odette Leroux. 2006.
Norval Morrisseau: Return to the House of Invention. Joseph & Norval Morrisseau. 2006.
Odjig: The Art of Daphne Odjig 1966-2000: The Art of Daphne Odjig, 1966-2000. B. Boyer & C. Podedworny. 2002.
But Is It Art? Darryl Dennis. Revision Quest. CBC Radio.

Spotlight – Indian Group of Seven

In 1973, the Indian Group of Seven was formed as a means for the founding members to support each other in promoting the work of First Nations artists as art, rather than simply as craft. Their goal was to have the world see First Nations works as art in the same way and at the same level as mainstream art. Although their actual name was the Professional Native Indian Artists, they were most often referred to as the Indian Group of Seven due to the major impact they had in raising the profile of the work of First Nations artists. The group included Daphne Odjig, Norval Morriseau, Alex Janvier, Joseph Sanchez, Jackson Beardy, Eddie Cobiness, and Carl Ray. Some refer to Bill Reid as the eighth member of the group as he sometimes joined the group in their joint exhibitions over the few years that the group worked together. Their last group exhibition was in 1975 in Montreal.

Chapter 7

The Road Forward: Forging a New Path

There is a spot in Lytton, B.C. where the Thompson and Fraser Rivers meet. One river is clear and one is murky, so when they come together they form one murky river. Despite their effect on each other, they are stronger together. First Nations people and non-First Nations people can do the same if we choose. Our paths are continually crossing, but usually we lead separate and distant lives. We sometimes meet and clash and then separate rather than coming together to strengthen all of our lives. This is the time to change.

Regardless of who you are, what your experience has been, or what you already knew - hopefully now that you have read *First Nations 101* you will have a better understanding of some of the many issues that affect the day-to-day lives of First Nations people. You may be asking yourself "what can I do to help foster positive change?" If you're not, then I am asking you to consider it – not just for First Nations people, but for Canada as a whole. It is clear that economic and social challenges faced by any person or group of people can also negatively affect others either directly or indirectly through higher social service programming, justice, or health costs. These challenges can result in higher taxes, competition for scarce resources, and poor relations between the two groups. Since I believe this, I advocate for change for all people facing social and economic challenges and for the disenfranchised, not just First Nations people. Most often, the direction of a society is focused on the economic growth of a country and its people rather than on what makes a strong country, both economically and socially. I don't believe that placing economics at the top of the list of priorities is in the best interest of anyone, not even those who continue to become richer at the expense of others, the environment, and the country.

It has taken many successive generations to bring First Nations people to the place we are today, so we cannot expect to create significant change within a short span of time. We face many challenges directly related to colonization and the residential school experiences, but we also have much strength upon which we can draw to foster positive change for ourselves as individuals, families, and communities. It is important to recognize that not all First Nations people are facing social or economic challenges. In fact, many of us are doing much better than our parents or grandparents did, both economically and socially. However, some of our relatives or friends may not be as fortunate and many are still facing multiple challenges. The underlying social problems must be meaningfully addressed in order to develop healthier individuals, families, and communities. This is not to say that all social problems must be addressed first, but they certainly must be addressed with the same commitment, resources, and support that economic issues are.

Whether we are non-First Nations or First Nations, we must all accept our responsibility for fostering positive change in the society in which we live. We must ask ourselves what we can do. Whether what we choose to do is large or small, it will all make a difference. When was the last time you donated funds or time to a First Nations' initiative, stood up against racist comments or acts, shared with others the truth about our shared history and First Nations issues, or held your local, provincial, or federal government accountable for their social and economic policies with your vote, by writing a letter, or direct action? Canada as a whole can be much stronger, safer, and healthier if its citizens hold governments accountable for the social and economic problems that arise for all people due to their policies, or lack of policies. We must insist that politicians think beyond the next election and implement ways in which to foster long-term sustainable change. We must stop being complacent. Once we do, we will begin to see positive change that affects us all, and then we will understand that we deserve and should expect more.

There are First Nations organizations across this land that are doing great work in the areas of health, justice, youth, families, and children. When will governments and other funders stop researching things to death and look to those who are already doing effective work? Why is it not as credible just because it is being done by a social service agency, because there is no research to back it up, or because it is not following some formal development or evaluation process? I believe the most important thing to consider is whether or not it is working. Who can argue with that?

Now, I encourage you to do something to help make things better for First Nations people and Canada as a whole. You can find ways to help that best suit your interests just by reading individual chapters of this book. I have identified problems, and some solutions. Many of these issues need advocacy, funding, letters of support, partnerships, or volunteers. At the very least, you can share some of this information with others, especially those who are misinformed or are making mistaken assumptions. You have already taken the first step in fostering positive change simply by purchasing and reading *First Nations 101*. Although I don't expect to earn much money, I have committed to donate one dollar from every book sold to the Native Youth Centre Endowment Fund in Vancouver, B.C. This endowment fund will be used in perpetuity to help the Urban Native Youth Association carry out its important work. You can find out more information at www.nativeyouthcentre.ca or www.unya.bc.ca. Thank you for being open-minded enough to read *First Nations 101*, and thank you in advance for any positive action you may take in the future.

The following pages contain lists that are practical, immediate solutions that can be worked on by individuals, groups, or governments. However, they will not happen without you and I working together, encouraging others to join us, and by making governments accountable to us all.

10 Things Everyone Can Do

1. Continually learn about the true history of First Nations people within Canada and the United States, and share that knowledge with others.

2. Continually hold federal, provincial, and territorial governments accountable for their policies, actions, and laws that lead to the widespread social and economic challenges that First Nations people continue to face. Write letters, send emails, sign petitions, attend rallies, and use your vote wisely.

3. Actively support First Nations social service organizations through volunteering, donations, advocacy, and partnerships.

4. Actively support First Nations political organizations through advocacy, partnerships, and volunteering.

5. Actively support the many First Nations singers/songwriters, cultural and language teachers, artists, service providers, videographers, educators, politicians, Elders, students, community workers, parents, and environmentalists who are focusing their work and efforts on strengthening our community.

6. Let your local news and entertainment television and radio stations and newspapers know that you want to hear and see more First Nations good-news stories, music, and events. Let them know that if they don't provide it, you will listen to, buy from, or watch other media that will.

7. Attend First Nations events with your children, friends, and family to learn more about and support First Nations people. Many events are open to everyone, not just First Nations people. Don't be shy or afraid to attend a pow-wow, concert, conference, or play.

8. Advocate for the immediate stoppage of the use of First Nations people and symbols to promote non-First Nations items, businesses, or sports teams. Write letters, send emails, and don't buy their tickets or merchandise.

9. Do what you can to stop acts of racism and bullying against anyone wherever and whenever you see or hear it. Let those who are being racist or bullying know that it is not okay; let the person who is being attacked know that you don't approve of it and will help if you can; and report acts of racism, hatred, and bullying to the proper authorities at work, school, or government or policing agency.

10. Don't appropriate our culture, traditions, or art. It is very disrespectful to see non-First Nations people doing our dances, carving our art, or running sweatlodge ceremonies. These things are often taken and used to make money and/or to fulfill a need for a cultural and spiritual connection for someone. Rather than take our traditions, I encourage you to find out more about your own heritage and honor the ways of your own ancestors.

10 Things First Nations People Can Do

1. Learn about and live the true traditional teachings of our ancestors which were based on inclusion of all community members, respect, spirituality, honor, and love.

2. Let go of the burden of your individual past as well as our collective past. Find ways to move beyond the anger, silence, shame, and anything else that is holding you back from the healthy life that you deserve. There are always opportunities for us to choose a better path; we just need to be open to recognizing and taking hold of them. That is what our ancestors fought for.

3. Encourage and support other First Nations people to make positive changes in their lives.

4. Stop the silence and the shame that are harming our families and communities by speaking out against all forms of violence, sexual abuse, corruption, discrimination, and other unhealthy behaviors.

5. Use your vote wisely. Don't vote for someone because they are your friend or cousin. We must all educate ourselves on the real issues and then vote for those who you know will work towards positive change for your community.

6. Decolonize your mind! This means letting go of all of the thoughts, behaviors, and beliefs that have been forced onto First Nations people since first contact and hold us back as First Nations people. Let go of negative thoughts about yourself and other First Nations people, believe in the strength of our people, not the challenges, and believe in and live by the traditional teachings of our ancestors. There are many other ways to decolonize your mind and life, but these are the most empowering things which can immediately change your life for the better and give you

the strength to challenge and change the rest.

7. Use the medicine wheel to help balance your life. We can use it as a tool to help assess the overall health of our families and communities, and to incorporate it into our daily lives to plan how we will achieve better physical, emotional, mental, and spiritual health.

8. Remember that more than half of our population is under the age of 25. We can no longer ignore our young people. Remember, they are the ones who will have to take care of us and our communities when we are older.

9. Remember that we are responsible for the next seven generations to come. We must make good decisions for ourselves and our communities no matter how hard they are to make. We must do this so that the generations to come will not continue to suffer as many of us do today.

10. Remember that we are a spiritual people. Despite what beliefs have been forced upon us or what any of us believe today, all of our traditional teachings and practices were spiritual in nature. They are the things that sustained our communities since the beginning of time and ensured everyone in the community was taken care of and respected. That is good enough for me.

10 Things the Government of Canada Must Do

1. Fully implement the United Nations Declaration on the Rights of Indigenous Peoples. This does not mean a vaguely worded commitment to review, look at, endorse the 'spirit of', or any other stalling tactic. Rather, it means immediately implementing the Declaration in partnership with First Nations people.

2. Honor all treaty, constitutional, and moral responsibilities. Quit using the court system to stall or stop living up to your responsibilities in the areas of treaties, child welfare, the *Indian Act*, First Nations women's rights, education, health, land claims, residential schools, and many other areas that have been stalled due to government actions or inactions.

3. Significantly narrow the poverty gap between First Nations people and other Canadians. It is an international shame that in 2010 Canada was listed in the top eight countries in the world while First Nations people within its own borders live in 78th position on the United Nations Human Development Index. Provide adequate funding for widespread First Nations healing, cultural reclamation, and community development initiatives.

4. Immediately fulfill your responsibilities to the survivors of Indian residential schools and their descendants as was promised through the Prime Minister's formal apology on June 11, 2008 in Parliament of Canada. This includes immediately reinstating funding for the Aboriginal Healing Foundation and the National Residential School Survivors Society, fulfilling responsibilities from the Gathering Strength Report, and providing adequate funding to widespread national healing, cultural reclamation, and community development initiatives.

5. Do not allow First Nations Bands or any land-based First Nations focused political organizations to assume financial responsibility for all First Nations people. Almost 60% of us live in urban settings and we want to continue to fulfill our responsibilities for child welfare, health, education, housing, and other economic and social programs in support of urban off-reserve First Nations people. We know best what our needs are and how to fulfill them. There is already severely inadequate funding for urban off-reserve First Nations people, transferring authority to Band Councils or any land-based First Nations focused political organizations will make it worse as they are also in desperate need of more funding.

6. Provide funding for a national urban off-reserve First Nations political advocacy entity that will be governed by urban off-reserve First Nations leaders as defined by urban First Nations people. This will help to ensure that there is meaningful and full involvement of urban First Nations leadership and organizations at all planning and funding tables. We do not want to be represented by anyone other than ourselves. This body must be funded at the same or higher level than the Assembly of First Nations as it will represent over 50% of the First Nations population.

7. Quit forcing programs upon First Nations people such as the Urban Aboriginal Strategy, as they do not work. Rather, provide funding to urban First Nations people through Councils similar to the Metro Vancouver Aboriginal Executive Council so that they can develop and implement strategic plans that will help to better support and empower urban First Nations people. Councils that are comprised of Executive Directors of major established urban off-reserve First Nations organizations are in the best position possible to know and address the needs of urban off-reserve First Nations people.

8. Make National Aboriginal Day a statutory holiday and promote it at the same level of marketing and funding as Canada Day or any other statutory holiday.

9. Put an immediate stop to the extraction of natural resources from our traditional territories until all land claims and treaties are entirely finalized to the satisfaction of all parties.

10. Quit being afraid to address these issues. Don't leave it for those who win the next election as that has never worked. There is very little to lose as a country and so very much to gain by doing something now.

10 Things Provincial and Territorial Governments Must Do

1. Pressure the Government of Canada to fully implement the United Nations Declaration on the Rights of Indigenous Peoples in partnership with First Nations people by formally supporting it through provincial and territorial legislatures and through direct pressure on the federal government.

2. Fulfill your responsibilities in relation to First Nations land claims, treaties, and constitutional rights.

3. Quit using the court system to delay or avoid fulfilling your responsibilities in relation to First Nations people.

4. Do not allow First Nations Bands or any land-based First Nations focused political organizations to assume financial responsibility for all First Nations people. Almost 60% of us live in urban settings and we want to continue to fulfill our responsibilities for child welfare, health, education, housing, and other economic and social programs in support of urban off-reserve First Nations people. We know best what our needs are and how to fulfill them. There is already severely inadequate funding for off-reserve urban First Nations people; transferring authority to Band Councils or any land-based First Nations focused political organizations will make it worse as they are also in desperate need of more funding.

5. Provide funding for a national urban off-reserve First Nations political advocacy entity that will be governed by urban off-reserve First Nations leaders as defined by urban First Nations people. This will help to ensure that there is meaningful and full involvement of urban First Nations leadership and organizations at all planning and funding tables. We do not want to be represented by anyone other

than ourselves. This body must be funded at the same or higher level than the Assembly of First Nations as it will represent over 50% of the First Nations population.

6. Quit forcing programs upon First Nations people such as the Urban Aboriginal Strategy, as they do not work. Rather, provide funding to urban First Nations people through Councils similar to the Metro Vancouver Aboriginal Executive Council so that they can develop and implement strategic plans that will help to better support and empower urban First Nations people. Councils that are comprised of Executive Directors of major established urban off-reserve First Nations organizations are in the best position possible to know and address the needs of urban off-reserve First Nations people.

7. Provide funding for a provincial or territorial urban off-reserve First Nations political advocacy entity that will be governed by urban off-reserve First Nations leaders as defined by urban First Nations people. This will help to ensure that there is meaningful and full involvement of urban First Nations leadership and organizations at all planning and funding tables. We do not want to be represented by anyone other than ourselves.

8. Quit appointing anyone you want to represent First Nations people and quit being afraid to stand up to First Nations people who are bullying their way into decision-making roles regarding First Nations issues and funding. You know who the true leaders are who know the issues, are ethical, and have the best interest of the community in mind. If you want real change, then change the way that you choose people to represent First Nations people when discussing issues and funding allocation.

9. Put an immediate stop to the extraction of natural resources from our traditional territories until all land claims and treaties are entirely finalized to the satisfaction of all parties.

10. Financially support First Nations arts and culture as a way for First Nations people to reconnect with their culture and traditions, not just as a way to attract tourists.

Acknowledgments

Writing *First Nations 101* would not have been possible without the support, love, and encouragement of Phil, Robin, Agnes, and many family, friends, and co-workers. Little did I know what I was getting myself into when setting out to include so much information in one book so that it would be an accessible point of entry for those who are interested in learning more about First Nations people – as well as our shared history with non-First Nations people. There are so many people I have met throughout my life who have shared information with me that eventually made its way into *First Nations 101*. Without their willingness to share their knowledge in order to help me learn, I would not have been able to write such an extensive book.

My children and I are honored to have been raised in the traditional, unceded territories of the Musqueam, Squamish, and Tsleil-Waututh Nations. Thank you for allowing us to live, work, play, learn, and practice our traditional culture in your territory. You have always made us feel welcome.

My absolute respect and gratitude goes to our First Nations ancestors who never gave up hope and fought against great adversity and over-whelming odds so that their descendants could learn their cultural and spiritual traditions – and to live a good life. Their strength and determination is a great inheritance that we must all acknowledge, celebrate, and pass on to future generations.

Visit www.firstnations101.com
to find out how to book a workshop or presentation,
when Lynda Gray will be in your area,
where you can buy *First Nations 101* or
how to order directly from the publisher,
and much more

www.firstnations101.com

PROGRESS ?

lyndatoon

GONE FISHING

About the Author

Lynda Gray is a member of the Tsimshian Nation and the Gisbutwada Clan (Killerwhale). Her ancestral roots are in Lax Kw'alaams on the Northwest Coast of British Columbia through her late mother Norah Gray (nee Wright) and her late grandmother Elizabeth Gulbrandsen (formerly Wright, nee Moody). She was raised in the Eastside of Vancouver and is the proud mother of two adult children: Robin Gray, a Ph.D student in Cultural & Social Anthropology, and Phil Gray, an established artist in Northwest Coast Tsimshian style. Lynda has been the Executive Director of the Urban Native Youth Association in Vancouver for the past four and a half years.